How to I
Money with
Rental
Properties?

Table of Contents

Chapter 1: Introduction to Rental Properties

Understanding the Concept of Rental Properties

Game of Investment and Income

Firstly, rental properties are not your typical properties. These are specially targeted for generating income more than dwelling purposes. As an investor, you purchase these properties with an intention to let it out and make some rental income over time, mainly for fending against fluctuations in the market. These can be, units like residential commercial properties that people lease out for usage, commercial buildings or even large apartment complexes that are rented for housing.

The key Players

In the world of rental property, there are three game players. You have the landlord, who is the chief regulator making sure the property stays up to par. Next up, there is the tenant or renter who leases or rents the property. Finally, a property manager comes into play when the landlord decides to hand over the maintenance of the property to a third-party manager.

Different Flavors of Rental Scenarios

Through a concise understanding, these rental units are typically leased out long term. But they can come in various flavours too. we can think of traditional houses, apartments, industrial spaces, or commercial outlets where the tenant pays a fixed monthly rental for an extended period of six months to a year or even more. Examples of short-term leases short-term leases includes vacation homes listed on Airbnb, and office spaces defaulted to co-working operators who rent affordably on a per-day or per-use basis. It pretty versatile once you understand how it works.

Investing in Rental property

Sounds rich right! So, I really think as an investor, it's good to focus on rental yield or annual rental return it would potentially provide. Some primary factors can hugely impact upon this. One of the main factors of purchasing rental properties is the budget and the amount of investment you're willing to make. Understand the point of how rental properties are different than flipping houses which are rehabilitated and sold at a significantly higher profit. Rental properties are long-term investments when you buy such a property, you intend to make your profits over time through operations, unlike flipping, which is time sensitive and is sold shortly after changes.

The Ideal Location

Ah, I know how you believe in the importance of location! In the world of rental properties, location heavily matters. Stable or increasing tendencies of the neighbourhoods can bring imminent strong demands, and this inevitably means great rent value. The gamble is to seek upcoming locations, appreciate well, and provide decent opportunities for tenants. So careful surveys pre-investment is a real deal.

To Furnish or Not

I know you love re-decorating houses, so here's something to perk your interest. You get to decide whether to provide your properties furnished or unfurnished; this might seem lackluster but know this understanding the requirement of tenants mostly defines revenue channels.

Responsibility of a Landlord

You also have to fix up plumbing or sort out some ill-wired connections. Ah, the sounds of labour-scary right. Instead of being occupied by rent, understand there come plenty of restrictions and duties attached to rental properties. You are obligated to meet housing code standards, address maintenance issues promptly, and respect the rights and privacy of the tenants you harbor.

Tenant's Role and Property Manager

Trust me, the property manager you assign would not even be welcomed to barge in at odd hours. They have to give well-reasoned prior notice unless it's serious as leakages or fire accidents; you have to remember there are strict rules in lease agreements necessity to familiarize with rental-property laws beforehand.

So, buddy gearing up for the world of rental properties sounded hard; honestly, it seldom is for entrepreneurs new to the scene. However, know if you strike it, the first right adds proper touch ups, cover the landlord's duties ideally, your investment might just turn exciting and fruitful. Bores become just stories when profit riddles are solved through experienced handling. You'd become a kind of god hand in developing passive income streams; now, wouldn't that make any hassle worth delving in?

On the bright side, a stable rental income is addressed as one of the main benefits that investors relish. Imagine having a consistent stream of money coming in from your property every month. Talk about a financial stepping stone to build wealth and reach financial freedom for everybody, right?

What's even more—with potential tax benefits, real estate investing often allows investors encompass numerous expenses to lessen taxes. Implying mortgage interest, property tax, operating expenses, depreciation, and even repairs can be held up for the guy's big deduction.

Another perk of owning a rental property is — take a guess depending on what you think … property appreciation. Yes, appreciation! Over time, the value of your rental property typically goes up, which might yield a nice profit when you finally decide to sell.

Now, tenants. Having someone else in a contract to take care of your property? Alright, that sounds like game show buzz to the potential investor! Because most often, they leave the property in better shape when tenancy concludes. Why? Everyone wants to retrieve their security deposit. That's a brainer!

Rolling deeper into our joy ride — thanks to leverage, owning rental properties allows investors to borrow money to buy the property. Too sweet to keep up, right? Here, part of the rental income goes to repay the borrowed money. And over some time, you start gaining reasonable money on your small investment. This leverage makes investing in rental property famously stand out. More to go? Increase in rent over time! Generally, rent tends to rise over time — itself being the smart strategy of pulling off with some astonishing profits. Especially in the resilient market locality. Trusted protocol has always been: buy investment property below market value. Keep up rentals aside and knock, knock jackpot of opening door to growing rental income starts. Candy coated out there then? Ohhh…wait my friend, investment logic shouts nothing easy comes out without its fair share of challenges. From costs and expenses to repair updates, they chew, smash, and splurge away a fair share of rental profit. Cue big advantage of buying real cash flows up in bargain to avoid such exceptions of unwanted surprise elements. If you've chalked up, the hunt worth prize thumbs joy notes of public traffic enjoying throughout all seasons

Speaking of kids? What am I talking about —scratch them instead, I meant damages by tenants can come rumbling loud stomping down the profits like scorned Thanos. Rule-toss ball among groups sometimes rents havoc beautiful enough to wish Star-Lord hadn't ambled fingers meddling poking up confusion straight at Thanos. Also, adverse legal altercations, remember having warned. From interpreting, tenant's rights lead to losing bets sinking money into ranted weeds flooded forgotten bowing sour goodbye tunes.

To slip up even further economic downturn serves a serious gut-wrench all developers eye on. Empty units gulp negative cash flows bereave ring extra drains into reserves pulleying financial crisis upon investments under watch. Barring personal partake, depending upon property managers, certainly hints throwing unintended trust spinning shaky wheels. Tending an experienced property manager too rich of a deal capable chirping may rattle worrisome result runoffs prioritized long down list clung haphazard fumble. Oh surprise furry ball, unexpected vacancies can swing all your savings right out the window. Bottle up dandy profit levels on beforehand before a property lune sneaks gliding in marching loneliness ahead.

How we are missing discussing limitations on liquidity! By definition, refers 'how much easily taking out the money invested peeping placed inside'. Unlike stocks bounced upon selling clicks, real, estates pack a road junkie tacked haul towards lengthier period mulling slowing transaction speed time.

Being encumbered, as invested having quit back early goose seeing off fingers squishing escape seeing underneath running deadlines framed without breaching down investment!

As uprooted breeches speed below tad limit, dealing with difficult tenants gusty zipping buckle over initial agreements serving bumpy textures scraping under premises billowing smearing sullen oil layers across trust.

Without wrapping up loud across billboard — tighter out underlying frameworks, according to zoning laws breed difficult twins sticking both easy way and out laying confused bricks molding beneath slogging scores resting down under law restrictions circling best picks.

The primary thing you need to know about the real estate market is that it encompasses various tangible properties. These properties include land, every physical structure attached to it - houses, buildings, fences, or even natural things like trees! Those thoughts of flipping a swanky urban duplex, becoming a landlord of a downtown market complex, or selling off those lush acres of passed down farmland all center around the real estate market. Remember one fundamental thing about the real estate market; it is typically divided into residential, commercial, industrial, and raw land. Residential deals with multi-faced dwellings like duplexes, vacation houses, townhouses, or even condos. Commercial real estate is all about business-related properties: malls, offices, shops; pretty much places business establishments conduct their operations. Industrial real estate, the way the name hints, refers to warehouses and industrial buildings. Lastly, raw land refers to any undeveloped property such as vacant lands, ranches, or outskirts farms.

Reasons to Embrace Real Estate

Now, you might be wondering, why the obsession with real estate? It is because real estate has immense potential, it offers a broad range of investment opportunities. There's diversity in the offerings, from buying a duplex to lease out to building a strip mall. Deciding to embark on this journey provides one significant advantage that can't be overlooked - the supply is limited! If price trends remain the same, take areas with high demand with a short supply usually observes marked price advances that makes property owners happy like kids in candy store. In periods when housing needs grow higher than available homes or land, the increasing prices pushes property-owners into pure bliss with the growth of their net worth.

One more fantastic thing about investing in real estate is predictable cash flow. For instance, if you're lucky to acquire some renters, you'll generate income every month - even during those money-loser tragic movies that Wall Street drops once in a decade. Think about it as a safety car is to an albino race whenever wild prices fluctuations crush equity markets.

Demand and Supply Law

Understand that just as it is in every other economical market - the law of demand runs wild here too: the housing market healthy depends on the temperature of buyers and sellers' moods. Buyers are desperate thieves searching and hunting while sellers interact as the generous givers - the ones who fulfill others´ needs. But the significant part - the one you've been waiting for - is that generally in this arena (hello dealers!), booming markets favour participants. They know the rules, and once the momentum flow their way, you would have armed yourself to grapple the backs of the spurting horn that economy sometimes morphs into. When your rented property spikes up due to demand or favorable government policy, you'll see your ballooning net worth.

Impact of Economy & Demographics

Real estate trends are greatly impacted by demographic and economic figures. Factors such as economic growth, employment rate, or big demographic shifts (baby boomers retiring, millennials deciding not to buy homes) have the horsepower to move the vast marketplace. However, dear friend, it's crucial to remind you that real estate takes time to sink in these market pulse changes - much slower than equity markets!

This economy coupling has some advantages. Property values and rental rates grow healthier during those rare warmed-up economic greenhouse periods, providing excellent returns. On the flip side, during devastating periods of economic blizzard or a 'Great flood of Pain' impactful event, things might walk contrarily, prices could deflate, or lenders might develop sweaty grip - taking loans could become tougher. Remember, continually adapting to market cues is like setting foot towards the path of prophetic crystal gazer.

At the close of today's friendly chatter, I can summarize our energetic conversation by confirming real estate is a lot! Limitless opportunities diversify risk-return profile to such levels that only a wise glance can give not a surprise tickle on your nose-side by this heavyweight of a sector.

Setting Realistic Financial Goals

The key to making money in any type of real estate investment, like rental properties, is really about setting realistic financial goals. You've got to know your numbers, pal. How much are you ready to spend on this property? How much do you expect to earn in return? These answers will be instrumental in decision making and shaping productive strategies. I'll explore upon them more considering they hint at the most pivotal concepts.

Understanding the realities of rental property returns, mate, is essential for financial goal setting. Take caution. While real estate can be a marvelous investment option with keen returns, it's not a guaranteed "get rich quick" scheme. There are quite a lot of factors in play, such it being potentially time-consuming, involving hands-on management, and depending on market ambiances. That explained, it's still worth your effort if you tread smartly. Even before you start searching for a property, you've got to articulate your desired return on investment (ROI). I'd suggest a minimum 6-8% annual return for a stand-alone house. But consider these nuances. For instance, multifamily properties like a duplex might pull in more. This percentage must be handy when hunting down rental properties considering ROIs widely fluctuate. A property might cost you $1 million and only rake in $60k/year.

And in another case, a location with lower cost could bring a similar $60k/year payout. For cash flow analysis, focus less on the overall investment and more on the ROI ratio - it's the latter that lands you to lucrative real estates.

Once you squirrel out a property in your desired ROI range, you ought to narrow down the specific costs associated with it. Rent is just one inflow (and the healthiest). Yet you've got to cross off expenses for regular maintenance, taxes, utility, insurance and whatnot, all nibbling at your gross income. I'd suggest having a reserve fund ready for those sudden, heavy-hitting replacements like roofs or HVAC units.

Smoothing all those out, your final profit is the net cash inflow. That's your property running you a positive sum at the end of it all. Quickly think of the down payment funds, the renovations - everything that aided set up this system. Subtract it merely and boom! You've got your Capital Gains! Remember them (possibly) being taxed based on short vs long term possession.

Now, our chat increasingly highlighting financial concepts could bamboozle you. Fret not! No one's asking you to turn an MBA overnight! Amidst good research, making tailored strategies, easy number crunching, and absorbing advice from this long-winded education-fest from me, you'd have carved half a path. Adding up a few numbers shouldn't spike a sweat with your masterful budgeting experience, amigo!

Experiencing it practically situates you somewhere to garner knowledge on property appreciation, tax benefits, and leveraging capital. And comprehending this trio nails right at the core of all real estate investments. Let me play sensei again and simplify them for you.

Property Appreciation, short and simple, is your property price's growth. It's expected, the markets fluctuating over time. Use it only as a bonus though, instead of making it slam dunk in your game considering unpredictability in market conditions.

Imagine this. You see this property sold for XYZ sum a few years ago. You throw in major fixes, enhance curb appeal, tend to minor lacks - sending the property's value looking skywards! Incrementally hiking the rent on yearly leases mirroring property value also fall under it wherever and whenever you can.

Tax Benefits doesn't really blurt out "perks!", bud! Turns out, it's a rather nifty retort if diligently picked up. Due to years-long depreciation triggered by wear and tear, property lifespan shortens that IRS paves ways to deduct rental incomes partially. This really makes ordinary Tax and Depreciation costs your armored characters in your Monopoly Money plays, how rad is that!

"Leveraging Capital" speaking finance, necessitates borrowing money to invest in something else. Imagine using lender's $100 knowing you will bag $105 back. Eventually, it could sequentially raise your "qualified for" amounts – remember, one should preferably use such calculated borrowing for your prime investments rather than leisure squandering.

And now, cherry-topping the sundae thought: having diverse rental properties boosts consistent profits funneling in. Rent out long-term, try vacation rentals, test out buy-flip rental properties, or trust turnkey rentals – everything brewed in the same pot, magnifying your "food" taste! Rome wasn't built in a day; steady diversifications are enrichments over time.

Lastly, grow connections within the industry as networking ultimately gives a sense of people preferring you over others for prospects on impending transactions, decreasing your search efforts dramatically. Heck, I wouldn't want you mailing me copies of rental law expectations though. Out of my league, partner!

So chin up, keep inquisitively researching, setting your believable numeric return values, tightly clutch real estate money inflow-and-outflow calculating, experience firsthand the triad concepts raising sturdy strategical implications. Time-tested these stand but take them with a grain of salt. If Rome wasn't built in a day, it couldn't have been brought down either, right? Embark on the journey of establishing your real estate kingdom that'll flourish currency in the modern economic ecology we live in!

Chapter 2: Types of Rental Properties

Residential Rental Properties

Residential rental properties, to put in simple words, are mainly detached and attached homes, duplexes, and condos which can be rented out to tenants. In other words, they are downright homes… rented out to a person, couple, or family looking to stay for a specified period.

"Rental properties are just passive income", you'd hear people say. Ha! if it ever offers passivity! On the contrary pal, active asset management is demanded. However, the dedication is worth it because the return it tends to give is amazing if done correctly.

An important parallel part surrounding this topic, mate, is property management. Indeed, obtaining desirable returns from rental properties starts with giving top-tier service to your tenants. Why dread the minor repairs or commitment when you are getting major value in return?

The critical parts, from tenant screening, lease negotiation, landlords' insurance to property maintenance, are but worthy costs and necessary evolutions in your landlord's journey. You can of course have a property manager to nudge these concerns away but let's just be real…no one can take care of your business the way you could.

On the other hand, don't forget these do come with responsibilities like any other business. You'd be facing laws around rent control, tenant rights and regulations so it's only wise to be aware and vigilant about these.

But if you look past the nuances, there's so much working in favor of rental properties. Let's start off with the biggest gain: rental income straight-away paying off many, sometimes most of your mortgage payables…ain't that just good business!

Apart from the financial aspects, you get to learn about investing and succeed on a big scale gradually. This segment of real estate deals majorly in 'playing your cards long', because long-term rental arrangements mean consistent returns, usually beating out bank saving or equity investments.

Tax benefits – don't get me started on this gem. Residential rental dictates expense deductions including property tax, mortgage interest, property depreciation, repairs cost and spanning to even travel expenses. Have you heard of two businesses where you can share your tour expenses with Uncle Sam?

Then come appreciation gains. Unlike most depreciable assets, property value is a growing graph projected unless external socio-economic factors act out. Quick cash isn't the expectation mantra but accumulated use and heightened value are definitely the attention grabbers here.

I remember offering leasing options using my property and my, the less oversight ties, pre-decided profit lines made things hassle-free, encouraging and consistent month after month.

Just to give you a veritable image pal, it's pertinent to understand the overall demands in rentals. You see, rental building demands are uniquely sector dependent with a country, region, city and sometimes street-specific vantage.

For example, in India, the burgeoning population and nuclear familial amendments demand humongous rental building requirements. Eastern and southern states of the U.S have similarly demonstrated consistent demands year-round.

Last but not least, challenges present themselves in any business area. It's everlasting so prepare yourself to be patient. Since when did reaching goals become easy, right partner? Undesirable vacancies, maintenance charges and tolerance management are just pointing on the learning curve. Having faith in oneself and persistence are the only counters, as rookie perspective implies.

However please, heed this seriously – only buy houses you yourself would imagine residing in. Subpar attempts of acquiring cheap properties just mount your problems creating a hot mess. Be strategic and move with clarity.

Above all remember – Investment doesn't always christen immediate returns but the learning acquired during the ordeal is the gift that keeps on giving.

Single-Family Homes

In essence, single-family homes are standalone houses while might be observed in almost any neighborhood. These are the traditional types of houses, ordinarily made for one family. Typically, this might indicate a property with a front, back, and possibly side yards, along with garage space as well. These can be listed in quite a wide spectrum of styles that encompass ranch styles, bungalows, cottages, and duplexes just to name a few. The homes usually have detached walls, meaning they do not share walls with any other residential building.

An advantage for investors / landlords leasing single family homes is their widespread appeal translating to potentially broader market stability. They can be found anywhere, with most tenants seeking the privacy and space these single-family homes provide. Significantly, single-family homes are often seen as more stable in value and typically appreciate well over time. This basically means if an investor buys a property today, years down the line its value is likely to go up, considering other factors like economy and location affecting the real estate market of course.

That being said, now that we've glanced over the basics of single-family homes, it is of utmost importance to understand the perks of investing in such properties.

One key advantage is that tenants usually stay longer in a single-family home. Typically, a family renting a single-family home is doing kindly because they seek stability and do not presume to be mobile shortly. Thereby, they are more apt to be something relating sub letters- in a way that they fulfill the property maintenance gaps that boarding property hires normally acquire.

Similar to dwelling life, one's home is their fortress, which countenances landlords to not often hold to do landscape design or handle minor problems as lessees take it upon themselves. This information is significant when observing investment property characteristics.

Likewise, with the turf sentiment, single-family property tenants are more inclined to mold the region enclosed into a neighborhood, that can't generally be accomplished in flats or apartments. However, on the downside- Being only able to count on one source of income from such types of properties serves as a drawback. If the tenants decide to move out or you get stuck with bad tenants, things can decidedly hold you back. Waiting periods for getting new tenants result in frustrating financial gaps for you as a property owner.

Also, sufficient and dependable property management is essential for single-family homes, notably when the owner doesn't reside in the vicinity to actively function in various circumstances. Of course, typically you can hire this out– but you have to keep this as an upfront cost in mind.

Analyzing all, solitarily owned homes are presumed to accumulate in an exaggerated vacancy density related to multi-family residencies. When you depend on a singular tenant for returns, in the counterpoint of when it's vacating is, it can render certain difficulties. Needless to mention such mortgage inconsistency component may oftentimes disturb the fiscal deliverable chart for an owner.

Still thinking all through, single-family homes are undoubtedly among the very popular tastes of investment possessions for both fresh and term state investors, and they are considerably simple to grasp. For instance, the ordinary house buyer comparably figures how solitary-family homes toil whereby other sort investments may be harder to comprehend.

It's key to note that the popularity and desirability of homes. Because these types of properties are in high demand, prices of homes tend to be more variable and respond to economic fluctuations. And keep in mind, though prices might take a hit during economic downturns, house prices tend to bounce back, often growing exponentially as the economy catches full speed. So as far as investments go, especially for those new to the real estate game, single-family homes remain and prove to be a solid option.

Overall, renting out single-family homes does come with its own challenges, however, understanding the property type and how to manage it efficiently, you can oversee prospective faults while maximizing your investment.

Nevertheless, always make sure that you do your research and make informed decisions. Keep your target market in mind; after all, they will be the pool you dive into during your renting phase!

Well mate, I hope our discussion today gave you some insights about single-family homes. It would only seem right if we discuss something else next as we're on the topic of rental properties. What about condos or multi-family homes? They're loads to discuss there as well. For now though soak in these facts. Who knows perhaps you'll soon be the proud owner of a single-family home or two or three!

You can picture these colossal properties as those hot-pink brick buildings you might have seen back in the days roaming the peach-colored downtown streets. Yup, that's right! Now, these leviathans present a sweet investment opportunity if you ask me. So, let's have a tête-à-tête about this, shall we? I like to see multi-family properties rental game just like baking a sizeable apple pie. The pie captures the concept of whole space while each slice is analogous to an occupied rental unit. As an investor, you bake the pie and sell it off in slices, or in this case, you own the property and rent out multiple individual units. Sounds profitable, right?

Guess what's more interesting? Multi-family properties can feather your investment nest pretty neatly. With various tenants chipping in different rent amounts, the total sum can ingeniously blossom into a neat monthly income stream. It more or less gives you a financial cushion. Lose one renter, no biggie, for you are not paralyzed and you still have all the others to beckon cash. So how do you find multi-pies—I mean multi-rentals... oops! Freudian slip, there. Start off by going starry-eyed in your real estate paradigm. Go asset-specific in your search under specifically for the likes: duplexes, townhouses, condominiums and apartment complexes. Before proceeding please consult with a real estate professional for the right direction and possibly locations. Actually, did you know, you have more control over the value of your property in multi-family investments? The value of such properties doesn't amazingly bake-in from market whims. Rather, it bakes-in, or maybe we should tune it down to valuations simmering on metrics like generated income, mechanical updates or applied management fees. You tweak the numbers there and you get to alter property's value for a top dollar!

Capital expenditure—don't be shaking. It's all simplified here for you. This essentially encircles the large expenses required to maintain the property or the 'revamping-spells' cash. Examples are cash spent on new roofing or the intercom system upgrades. In multi-family real estate, prepare for a higher CapEx due to heavy wear and tear from multiple families.

Hold on though—there's always a silver lining. These high CapEx occasions shoot a few bonuses points your way with a chance to increase rent. "But the roof engulfs me better," the renters would say. You get to toss up a small rent increase with more appreciated benefits. Ultimately you chalk down depreciations on your income taxes, remember the crackerjack principle behind taxing—taxes offset against earnings, affecting investor's clarity of wealth health, the bonafide Net Operating Income (NOI,) and valuation.

Hmm, management cost and effort are something I know you want to ask about. And, the laughs on me if I won't cough out the hairball. Multi-family properties churn more management load and cost more cheese—'props' time, costs, and even legal expenses as well. Any landlord with enough renters embarks on a private 'logistics juggler' odyssey—it's always fun until you miss a personnel query. Well hello, property & management companies to the rescue for a commission! Furthermore, finances available for multi-kin investments bear meatier, perks-laden financing deals even for beginners. Meanwhile, big capital down your way pairs sucker-punched interest rates rising further. Get it? At larger scales debt service ratio just roll benefits to the bank as you feed mortgage lenders with happy returns.

What about the hypes and downs in rentals? Truthfully, my downplay has been high during significant-market-pulls. Transaction costs are mountain riding with your stepping stones as banks try and surf more mortgage rates. Quite outrightly, there's always some cool fine cleaning-up strategies like buying homes directly leveraging data, relationships with fix-and-flip investors, bidding sharks…and more!

Vacancy rates—at some point surely tenants will move out—done with lease, moving city, relocating or take your pick. Did we slide to pitfalls? Unusually high rates call for troubled waters but syncing leasing tenants and managing rental properties is an art of its kind, mastered with practice.

Another glimpse into scale: Multi-family investments open various portals into playing scales around various specifications, a beneficial investment move. Fear of being entrapped in one, let's say 4-room palace. Not if you put a kaleidoscope to it and view each room as opportunities—and lo and behold, you could procure four revenues and not just one!

Whoops, can't close off without courtship invites! Neighborhood courtship affects rental prices & frequency of rentals, upkeep needs, turnout & quality of applicants besides affecting lender term prospects too. You don't want tenants skipping later, penning up bad nerves, penning negative areas around your properties that spook potential leads-ish away.

Finally, to many jumping ship singles' arena to multi-family scene smells triumphant. Perhaps louder voice on the table belong to multi-renting adepts cruising these challenges and flipping skills like flipping pancakes in pure sweet profitability spectacles. However, dexterity exercised is mastery earned—investments spinning multi-dialects talk around multi-front works sooner or later.

Condos and Townhouses

The Condo Guide

Let's start with condos. The term 'Condo' comes from 'Condominium,' often misunderstood as a type of building; however, it isn't about built shapes. Condo, fundamentally, is any housing unit situated within a larger property that is owned by an individual.

How do I describe it? All right, say you're checking out an apartment building. Each flat within that building can be a condo if sold to different individuals. It's sort of like a pizza. The whole pie is the apartment building, and every pizza slice can turn into a condo. Cool huh?

Owners of condos technically own their units but share ownership of common areas, including the parking basement, garden, or the building's roof with other residents. You have to pay a monthly owners association fee paid towards the shared spaces' maintenance. These condominium communities could either be apartment complexes or detached houses; whatever tickles your fancy!

A standout for condos is there's management that handles fixing up common spaces: workout rooms, swimming pools (if any), sidewalks, to mention but a few. Sounds relaxed, no?

Fun with Amenities, Friend—Cumbersome Rules Not So Much

Now on the icing, friend, condos offer a lifestyle filled with accessibility to desirable amenities, from gyms, swimming pools, saunas, party rooms, and concierge services all under one roof. Is it starting to sound luxurious, huh? Perfect for professionals who enjoy a serviced and fuss-free living. But here's the thing – some folks don't find the idea appealing, and you know why? The homeowner's association (HOA) rules may take away a sense of ownership. A condo environment is replete with rules – no loud music after certain hours, regulations on pet ownership and so on. That adds another good addition to the pros and cons to think of when considering your rental options, buddy.

The Study in Townhouses

Moving on, let's now strike the chord: Townhouses! Wondering how they differ from condos? Strap in, buddy. Despite appearing similar physically, these narratives diverge as different chapters. A townhouse epitomizes the charm of both worlds from single-family houses and condos. They describe ownership structures that are quite different from condos.

Picture townhouses, also referred to as row houses; as multi-level terraced houses, they usually have only one or two shared walls. Yep, you've got more privacy, bro, and of course, you aren't sharing too many walls.

What's exciting, just like condos, townhouses too offer shared amenities especially if they're part of a Homeowners Association (but no elevator rides with noisy neighbors thankfully!). A connected layout enables shared maintenance, limits your yard work, and still offers a decent, personal, outdoor space. Sounds sweet, doesn't it?

And just like standard houses, townhouses often come in two-story formats. You own both that piece of ground that your townhouse sits on and the structure itself - the inside and the outside. It sounds very similar to single-family homes, magic!

Getting a Hang of Homeowners Association Policies

Before trailing off, a nugget on the Homeowners Association (HOA). It's involved in both condo and townhouse deals but a heads-up, the HOA ain't a breeze. They levy monthly fees for maintenance services and present sometimes strict house rules. Not much like, you have to paint your door a certain color, more like keeping pets, noise limits, on-street parking restrictions, all stuff intended to maintain a civilized ambiance. Note friend, breaching these policies usually follows with financial penalties.

If you're considering pouring your investment into these

spaces, hope the picturesque idea of condominium and townhouse living spaces intrigues you. Both condos and townhouses offer mid-ground opportunities for those who can't seem to wrap around ultra-urban condos or suburban detached houses. But remember, herein too prowls restrictions that you, like age-old adventures, have to wrangle for surrendering a fulfilling gain.

Be assured it's viable moving from theory to material reign when you deliberate the advantages and disadvantages – with a traditional, laid-back essence in condos or more exclusive, flexible vitality dwelling townhouses.

Whatever the narrative, bear the salient jewel, these are handy pathways to home or investment reality long before entirely distanced single-family homes remains a dream in tall castles; the prices speak wonders! I'd debunk that in the next such meet and greet.

Commercial Rental Properties

First things first. When I talk about commercial properties, what comes to your mind? Huge office buildings in the heart of downtown, right? Close, but not quite. It's more than that. The category of commercial real estate does include office buildings. But, it also encompasses shopping centers, apartment complexes, warehouses, restaurants, medical buildings…you name it. If it's income-producing property for business more likely than not—it's commercial real estate.

Considering Commercial Rentals

Ready to roll your sleeves up? Awesome! Before you decide to dive head-first into the commercial property pool, though, you got to understand a few basic norms about the investment.

Notice the Bigger Initial Investment

Are you sitting down? Good, because here's a small shock for you—commercial properties typically cost more than residential ones. I told you, right? Not only are you often looking at larger buildings, space, or land, more like an upgrade from a small house in residential to big buildings in commercial.

Think long term

Commercial properties also don't flip as quickly as residential properties. There's a ton more that goes into opening a business compared to moving into a home. So, keep that patience because tenants' longer-term leases mean that in many of the calculations, the extra upfront cost makes sense in the long run.

Greater Potential Income and Stability

Now, here's some comforting news, though: commercial properties usually mean greater income potential, more stability, and fewer risks. Businesses tend to stay put and wanting to stay there for the long haul. Once set up, it's a pain in the neck to move an entire commercial operation!

Commercial Real Estate Terms to Know

Now, before stepping your foot into the commercial property game, it's essential to be familiar with certain terms/terms used by industry insiders—like the Net Operating Income (NOI), the capitalization Rate (the cap rate), and the Cash on Cash metric. Knowing these will help you to determine the viability of your investment and health of your portfolio.

Understanding the Types of Commercial Real Estate

Okay, now that got what it takes to invest in commercial real estate clearer let dive a bit deeper to look into specific types of commercial rentals:

Office Space

Classic concept, right? Yes, it's that world where 9-5 simply does not exist. These properties are business-oriented spaces usually in high-density downtown areas or suburban office parks—either rented or were fully owned by the businesses.

Industrial Spaces

Talk massive square-footage here! Industrial rental spaces run the gamut from warehouse facilities, shipping and distribution centers, refrigerated storage areas, and larger flex spaces that allow for both office and industrial uses in the same area. Usually, they operate on a Business-to-Business (B2B) model rather than a business-to-customer (B2C) blend.

Retail Spaces

Ah, shopping centers! Whenever retail spaces come in mind, shopping and every type of retail operation under the sun strike hard. From mom-and-pop shops to the big guns. Different types speak differently when it comes to demand and how profitable they can prove to you as an investment. The only looming factor will be; considering the area and potential client base when choosing what kind of retail to invest in.

Multi-family/Apartment Buildings

Well, well, that's my favorite on the list and arguably the most passive investment type. It refers to any kind of residential property that can accommodate more people and these typically offer renters studios up to three-bedroom suites. Yet, there is a pair rule; apartments six units and meaner commercial and lesser than six imply a residential property.

Do know investing in commercial spaces can indeed tool your portfolio up! Take the perks like higher leasing rates, triple net lease advantages, and stability into account. However, get that finding a lucrative deal you have to sweat off and deep pockets are kind of requisite too!

Believe, some of my best investment encounters were on properties that were "hard to sell." But then my friend, unicorns do exist, especially in the case of commercial real estate moments. Keep looking in the concrete jungle in a chance to stumble across real estate gold!

Office Spaces

What Are Office Spaces?

To start with, office spaces are commercial properties leased to businesses and enterprises. They come in an array of silver linings – you'd best believe it! They are as diversely amazing as that mini rainbow above waterfalls! From haute small settings suitable for creative startups, through to colossal skyscraping lookout towers that house established institutions, office spaces come tailored to a myriad requirements and preferences, guarantor of your best value for bucks.

Different Types of Office Spaces
Traditional Office Spaces

Now, before the clime changed by the advent of all the Tech Titans and Crazy Creatives, we principally had what's called Traditional Office Spaces – your regular Norma Jean. Typical features? These spaces often box private offices, conference rooms, a reception area and probably some additional storage.

They are commonly found unadorned, giving the lease consummate freedom to dial their unique preferences right into every nook and cranny.

Shared Office Spaces

Faced with the wave of change brought about by startups and SMBs (that's Small and Medium-Sized Businesses by the way), alternative office setups coined Shared Office Spaces swung into highlight. These guys swapped a lot of private cube with common room facilities like meeting rooms, reception services, and business machinery. Best guess? They christened it shared because businesses could nuzzle under the sheet of offered services. Very genius save, right? Freelancers, self-employed persons, and the occasional SMB that prefers lower responsibility levels are comfy nesting in them too!

Coworking Spaces

Along came another charm - the Coworking Spaces. Your friendly little commune where people from different professional backgrounds, interests, and companies work independently yet synergize on a healthy shared workplace ethos. Colorful open-seater tables, a loft of themed private offices, meeting rooms running paa-paa-paa can catch your eye. Oh, almost forget the snacks in the pantry - sure to woo you!

Executive Suites

Then the current trends segued in an electric sensation - the Executive Suites. Executive suites, for some reasons, carry around an elegant business-alto sex appeal blended with a silver of cozy homeliness. Essentially, they sculpt suave private office centers installed with premier services like personal reception, meeting rooms and office equipment. Sweet score for established businesses that prefer to slurp on served-the'-pay services while still raking high private facilities, space and service quality.

Virtual Office Spaces

I can't sit out without noodling in our extraterrestrial variant: The Virtual Office Spaces. Well, it's neither buzz sound nor hot air! Variable businesses - more especially International focused ones, largely run the race with clear eyes to bring down outlays for physical office space, sidestep lengthy leases, dodge steep bills while repping swell administrative support and corporate familiarity.

Benefits and Challenges

So, like every property, office spaces carry their angelic white card and - of course - the rogue side! On the bright flip, good investors would leverage:

Higher Returns: It's, most times, very tenable to prime in and lock them tender green bucks. Office spaces more than often run on more predictable cash-flow and long-term deals, compared to residential lease degrees.

Better Property Management: Rare to uncover office spaces primps placed under substandard maintenance care. They are usually managed profoundly. Well hopefully!

Retail space is basically property owned solely with the intent of earning income from sales made on location. We swoosh past shopping malls, small stores in the city, or larger establishments in downtown areas, but how many of us look at these bustling locations as potential gold mines? Maybe it hadn't even crossed your mind before, but honey, let me tell you—it certainly is a reality.

Pend me your ear, bud. Thinking of becoming a landlord but not interested in dealing with rowdy grad students hosting house parties, or endlessly calling you about the broken porch light? Consider submerging yourself more into the realms of retail space.

What is a Retail Space?

First thing's first; let's define retail space. This is literally any property designed to be used to sell goods or services. Look around. We're often surrounded by retail properties: the fast-food outlet you frequent (shh, "secret calories" don't count if no one knows), the boutique store (yes, the one with your desired shirt always out of stock), even the posh side of town with its yoga studios and endless coffee shops.

Why Rent Out Retail Spaces?

OK, buddy, here's the million-dollar question—why should one decide to get in on the retail space investing game? It surely isn't all sunshine and rainfall, right?! Well, like any risk, it comes with its degree of complexity, but boast potential rewards such as high rental income and long-term leases.

Operating expenses – including maintenance, utilities, and taxes - are often also - cover your excitement – managed and paid by the tenant! Quite a magical lease agreement (also called Triple Net Lease or NNN). Besides that, retail spaces provide keen and serious investors a chance to join their city's business community possibly, with a swanky property location to boot.

What Types of Retail Spaces are There?

Alright pal! Now you're brimming with curiosity: "What types of retail spaces are there, and how do I dive in?"

Why, there is a pool-party of options in this segment. Each category of retail property provides unique features and revenue opportunities. To keep it a little above water, here is a closer peep through the looking glass:

Strip centers: Oh boy, have you seen those smaller, local neighborhood premises, usually spotted with diverse retails like bakeries, barber shops, takeaway (that favorite pizza joint?), and maybe a workout studio? Generally simple designs and readily available parking make them a draw for local residents.

Community retail centers: You notice those 'wannabe superstar' stores housing culinary hubbubs, gigantic department stores, or intermediate sized spaces. The community center is where they reside; They tend to pull beacons from a larger radius compared to their strip-center counterparts.

Regional malls and Power centers: Think sheer revenue shells encased in enormous malls, including shopping Meccas like Macy's, Bed Bath & Beyond, and their sizably leased, large chicken" counterparts from the grocery world such as Costo or Home Depot.

Pad sites: These are those particularly snipped off and eagerly desired plots of land at the corner of a bustling storm of human traffic which is perfect for national chains or drive-thru seeking to prey on high visibility.

Mixed used retail: Envision an artisan cocktail of commercial spaces, services, offices, residences, sometimes even perfectly blended in one building or community.

No matter which corners of this vast playing field you decide to explore, remain remindful that tenants of these properties are often economic players with shifting priorities. Changes challenging their industry dictates can impact rent promptness or even their very presence in your property.

By far taking retail spaces by its antlers involves skill, risk but notable rewards. Whether this branch of real estate is your sophisticated battle-winner would be determined by several factors: the practical know-how on each retail space type, your financial capability, association factors like the local township, even your ability to go full throttle with the changing/current retail industry scenario.

Industrial Properties

Real estate is a powerful platform for wealth, and everybody knows it. But incorporating industrial real estate into your portfolio might seem like tricky business at first. Despite the intimidation, in truth, investing in industrial properties offers tremendous potential for high returns. And hey, aren't potential high returns why we decided to go down this rabbit hole in the first place?

Can I tell you something? The beauty of industrial space

investment lies majorly in its sturdy leases. Unlike residential leases that run from month to month or year to year, industrial properties frequently operate on multi-year terms - often between 5 to 10 years. No seasonal turnovers or semi-annual resigning here; rather, the rate of leases ensures a consistent and predictable flow of income. You dig it?

Here are a few types of industrial properties causing the swings in the investment world; ready to dive in?

To begin with, bulk warehouses or distribution centers rent the most space of the industrial real estate family. Think companies such as Amazon, IKEA, and FedEx – businesses that need to store massive amounts of product before they're shipped to retail spaces or customers. One of the things to note is these guys are pretty size-specific. The sheer size of bulk warehouses typically ranges from 50,000 square feet to hundreds of thousands of square feet. Many also possess truck doors where goods can be loaded and unloaded directly.

High-street buildings aka 'light industrial sites' cater to companies executing numerous facilities – from research, product production, and service businesses such as car repair, plumbing, or gym studios. Here you'll find properties specifically designed to accommodate logistics of loading/unloading offers, as machine storage is commonplace here. Taking note, however, one key thing that differentiates the light industrial from its bulk warehouse brother is this – utility intensity

Alright, flexible industrial sites serve the purpose of both warehouse and light industrial buildings. Divided into two sections - one dedicated to productions and another allotted for offices or direct dealings with consumers – they're way of combing variety and utility into space. So, somebody running a bakery could keep all their equipment on the production side while serving customers in a storefront setup on the other side. A tad ingenious go-around if you ask, right?

Did you know that Truck terminals provide spaces for the loading and unloading of trucks? Many services rent these spaces for only a fraction of a day. Hence what you need to know is this - unlike the many-year leases which the impressive bulk warehouses offer, truck terminals host brief turnaround times. But watch out - though the leases seem shorter than a summer fling, the spaces fill out so quickly information doesn't barely seep out.

Particularly different from the other main classes of industrial rentals are data or e-commerce centers. Box-breaking it by becoming conveners garner steam, data centers facilitate digital usage; including online sales, internet searches, cloud storage, communications, among many others. Securing an affinity with major tech companies, urban proximity determines their location – so don't go ahead planning an internet-free vacation around these ones. Jokes aside, watch brands as Amazon and Google major in providing data housing. With our ever-digital age, these buildings offer a slice of the real estate interest that current and future developments present. Although pricey, they often offer ample opportunities and lure entrepreneur veins through investment options which space as much as user-directed.

Chapter 3: Analyzing Market Trends

Conducting Market Research

Analyzing Market Trends for Rental Properties
Know Your Market Basis

Before you even begin, it's mega important that you're comfy with the land factors; those influenced by social, economic, geographical or government cheese.

For instance: tax regulations, population demographics, crime rates, local employers, community facilities, transport links or future developmental plans. Most authorities/public bodies have websites chock full of such intriguing specifics.

Demand and Supply Dynamics

Hit those journalistic instincts, mate! Tally the demand-supply markers on rental properties, making especial notes on most desirable properties – location, number of bedrooms, pet-friendly, off the street parking… You get the dispatch!

You can seek these findings generally online or observe the vacant properties, rental prices and respective periods each property was on the market. Procure these factoids to corner your prospects spot-on and tail rental rates that keep both you and your renter chipper.

Stay Legit with Legal Stuff

Study the local laws- nothing's worth carting a cart-load of legal hitches. You'll need astute advisories of laws governing rent control, safety compliance, tenant-landlord rights and eviction.

Meet the Competition

Once you've dispatched in your homework, well sit smug or keep grooving! The big fellas globally scribble continuous rental advisories on cities, key growth cum demand areas or rental averages.

Get your grasp here, it's real astounding on how that catapults your rental self-gauge. Add ongoing feedback from the octopus on the street [aka rental agents], they're an outpour with flowing rentals and clients' manifold behavioral delights.

Moreover, comparative marketing analysis [real estate comparable], again leans rich – pricing rationalization and client behavior grasps become valuable.

Sky's the limit with data analytics, enabling you capturing that acute pulse.

Loop Job Market & Economy Trends

Economic health triggers numerous factors that send those ripples off to population demographics [meaning: your potential tenants] like job proficiency, income ranges, mortgages- afford abilities.

Hook this ensemble with data records and considerate conversation with polite ground people there - that sure reels in some market juju!

Understanding Population demographics

Race a look at the folks demographics [age range, familial status, jobs, employed students et al], the factors are expansive.

Now bridge that to leverage into an optimal clientele genre. For instance - targeting toward young couples/families, gear your property for child friendly ergo; or smart singleton student homes pitched in high student density precinct.

Media Visibility

Sure fishing unassuming renters won't slice-off profit mounds. Jump the punch-train; network those social and commercial outlets to maximum optimization.

Rent periods fickle through standard calendars but pitching the correct property appeal on that sharp individuality - now that's visibility, right buddy?

Identifying High-Demand Areas

Why Market Trends?

Your Aunt Martha might tell you "investment is all about gut feelings." But keep sentimental notions for another day. When it comes to real estate and the rental property world, relying on guesswork is not encouraged. Getting serious means carrying out systematic research and analysis on market trends. In other words, say hello to facts, figures, and measurable factors. It saves us from those nasty investment disasters, of course.

Now you might wonder "What is a market trend?" Don't be afraid to ask the simple things, because these simple questions build up to the big conclusions. Simply said, market trends are the directions in which the market is going for a certain type of product or service.

It tells everything from ups and downs in the market, where it's heading, to what you-as an investor- can expect in the future. It sounds like a walking stick that we all need.

Rent Trends

Tackling rental properties specifically, we should underline Rent

Trends, AKA how rental prices move. Ups-downs, sideways, you got the theme again– tracking the trend here can be pivotal for your rights as a landlord to increase the rents accordingly or even sell your property.

So, it's no rocket science to sensing market trends. It's just being proactive, blending in the environment, doing some research, and figuring out your next move before stepping in.

Evaluating Market Trends

Sounds fancy right? But, hey, it is lot easier than you think it is. Start simply by looking at amount of and types of buildings that are under construction, have been recently completed, and planned projects to be built in the near future in a region.

More projects sprouting indicates booming demand and solid growth prospects. Websites like local papers, realty sites, city authorities or regional media outlets would provide a full play-by-play action of the neighborhood.

Next drill down into specifics like demographics, school quality, local economy, and amenities. The local crowd and community hold rich insights. If it's families in the area = larger homes, students = more rental demand, wave of newcomers and tourists = long term Airbnb rental opportunities. You get my jest, right? Also, keep an eye on the local economy – Job growth, stability, predominant sectors, flock of companies, existing talent pool - everything plays into property demands.

Moving on, time to watch retail trends - Record any superstores, food chains sprouting, big brands flocking in or even indie outlets gaining traction– All of it indicate a strengthening neighborhood.

Look for Trends-within-trends: Factor in infrastructure developments which also denotes area progress, like Access to public transport, highways, local amenities and connectivity to hospitals, essential spots;

Phew, too much info-digging, am' I right? But in reality - The more signs we locate, the stronger our predictions on where the pendulum is swinging.

Right on the Money

Okay so, you've done all the marking, checking, tick-boxing steps above but wait! It's not show-time yet. As we discussed before, ain't' there more factors counting in for the investment decision?

Affordability is right on top – Make sure the property is within your spending limits and mortgages won't leave you ridden in debt. Price to rent ratios or the median home prices against the median rent is a handy check – it tells you whether to sign for it, rent it or wave it a 'Goodbye!'. If the prices-to-rent ratio < 20 = It's cheaper to buy a home than to rent in that particular area, and vice versa. It's such a myth to lock in any 'Single Right or Wrong market' conceptions. Each offers both advantages and shortcomings. We have markets with low property values versus high rental yields, and then pricey-classy neighborhoods with high demand and great long-term appreciation. There isn't a perfect solution baked for all. It's about understanding and playing along with the demand-supply takes of people and places.

Rely also on third-party analytics, consultancies and user-friendly software tools - as Reinhard Gehlen, once said "Information is power". It maps market niches, sheds light on forecasts, rental comps and more to your resourceful benefit.

Long story short, key on "analyzing market trends" is equal to knowing right – content, time, place - of an investment decision. If mastered, it saves us from bad deals, cheers to great returns all the while witnessing property goals turning to successful projects. Remember – it's all in knowing where to look and move based on the signs. After all, "The best investment on Earth is earth."
— Louis Glickman. Happy property hunting, partner!

Determining Rental Rates and Occupancy Rates

3.3 Determining Rental Rates and Occupancy Rates
Location, Location, Location

You've doubtless heard this Realtors favorite mantra - location everything. But how does this transpose to determining rent?

Well, look, the environs really shape the desirability of your property, which, let's put it this way, markedly influences how much people are willing to shell out for it. A swanky uptown pad? Big bucks. A rustic rural dig? Less extravagance. Get the drift? Flex your inner Sherlock and research comparable properties in your area.

Weigh into Market Conditions

This is another juicy chunk to gnaw at. Woo-hoo! Let's sink our teeth in. See, my guy, market conditions swing like a funky pendulum. What's a juicy plum right now could be an everyday orange tomorrow or vice versa. Getting elbow-deep into market research has got to be staple for you, my busy friend. Latch onto buyer and renter behavior patterns; bite onto financial and demographic tendencies. Learn to gobble the ebbs and swells of the market; they'll draw out educated rates for your property.

Evaluating Your Property

So, let's chat about your investment property itself. Wowzah, it can influence the rental rate! Are we on the same page? Cool bananas! Aspects like the size, condition or available amenities of your rental all act as a big fat magnet (or not) to potential clients. Look around! If your property is bigger, better, bling-ier (nothing like making up words, eh?), Bump. Up. That. Rate.

Pricing Strategies

Ah, perhaps my numero uno slice! Moderation and strategizing. Nothing capsizes interest faster than bloated or nutty low rates, right? You get me. A rate too sky-high will swipe off your rental from consideration before quicksilver. Too bizarro low and peeps will wonder, "Hey! What's really the catch, right?" So, balance it out, will ya?

At the end of the day, understand that fair pricing automatically reaps timely payments, steady rentals (ah, the win of max occupancy rate), and high tenant retention. Knockout punch, isn't it?

Computing Occupancy Rates

Got your prop ready for rental? Bravos! But how will this deal turn up dandy if you haven't cracked that code to predict your occupancy levels? Not to leave you staring blankly, here we go. News is, a relatively uncomplicated equation helps us chums calculate this gnarly number:

(Occupied Days / Total Rental Days) x 100

Sum it up, multiply by 100. That number shot up is your occupancy percentage for the period checked. Pure genius, right? Big Caveat Alert: This can careen madly. Time of the year; differences between places, longer-term rentals versus nightly, weekly, or monthly rentals; average rent throughout the year, etc., all tango fiendishly into the equation. So, strap on your thinking caps, mate.

Real talk though - you championing maximum occupancy rates doesn't make universal sense. Stunned? Consider this – running a totally booked-out, bottom-dollar rental biz could knock off profits from a lesser occupied fat-pocket property. To profit from it, crisscross it well.

So, in our whisky-Jenga journey of sussing market trends for rental properties, sweetly analyzing rental and occupancy rates sounds like scrumdiddlyumptious best practices, right?

In then, to astutely determining market rent, lining out a shrewd pricing game, tailoring your rental to the demands of your customers, and learning to mesh occupancy rates alongside your off-peak and peak times. Circling back, my real-estate gladiator, understand that best-game pricing policies and occupancy rates engage to give longevity, prosperity, and sustainability to your business. Taking these factors rockabilly will return you clouted considerations and comfort in pricing your rental property.

Recognizing Potential Growth Areas

Let's get right into this real estate roller coaster!

Neighborhood Growth

Just like the way to capture a great picture is to go where the light is, the secret to great property potential can bucket down to—`Location, location … Wait for it… location!`

Let's bring that sentence to life. An up-and-coming neighborhood can make all the difference when it's about making bank with your investment. Consider elements like rapid population growth, declining vacancy rates and increasing income levels of residents. All these factors can scream that the neighborhood is in high-demand.

Moreover, pay notable attention to zoning laws. Think about it: special allowances could mean there's room for conversions or expansions, offering plenty of revenue generating potential.

And did I mention the absolute goldmine you could be sitting on with convenience at arm's length? Yes! Chop it down to simple elements, my friend—proximity to amenities like transit, airports, supermarkets, schools or universities. Remember, renters love convenience and are even willing to pay a premium for it!

Property Improvements

Second on our stroll, we come across Property Improvements. Rental properties don't usually come picture perfect and that's where the magic happens—this can be your chance to add value.

Basic updates such as new paint, improved landscape, fresh appliances and remodeled kitchens or bathrooms can exponentially add value.

Let me put you in this frame. John bought a rundown apartment for a competitive price. After giving it some needed love, he's now pulling in double of his projected rental income. The lesson here? Pick up dyed-in-the-wool flips and cherry-pick the areas to improve for a major bounce in property value.

Property Utilization

We're onto the third room—`Property Utilization`. Simply put, your property might sport rooms or spaces that can be motioned towards different uses—They might turn into money-spinning conduits to garner maximum rental income! Transforming a basement into a small apartment or configuring an attic into an exotic bedroom are textbook instances of pressing squeezed spots into commercial areas.

Additionally, consider flipping hybrid uses for your property. Cargo building into apartments or a turkey farm into single-family homes more often becomes brilliant in facilitating skyrocket returns on investments.

Economic Indicators

Lastly, knock-knock—it's our final room for familiarization—my good friend, Economic Indicators. Be owl-eyed about knowing trends in the job market. Strong local growth can potentially draw renters to neighborhoods. Likewise, observing positive migrations, reduced taxes can connote promising harvests returning from investments you seed in property.

Just keep in remembrance, my go-getter friend, that keeping your eyes open, understanding the indicators and wagering smart chess moves can let you end up with endless possibilities—royale as how your dreams have it!

Chapter 4: Financing Options for Rental Properties

Traditional Financing Methods

4.1 Traditional Financing Methods: Let's Go Basic

First off, let's start with traditional financing. Now, these methods that we're about to discuss aren't labeled 'traditional' because they're old or outdated. No, no! We call them traditional simply due to the sheer value, and pretty much solid viability, over extended periods. I mean, god, how can you go wrong with something that's successfully endured the test of time?

Bank Loans

The first idea that probably comes to your mind when someone mentions 'traditional financing', is good old bank loans. A lot of folks see banks as their go-to one-stop shop. Guy, you can rely pretty solidly on banks. You've got your fixed-rate mortgages, adjustable-rate mortgages, and so on. You drop your application, do your documents shuffle, and tada, they process the loans. Granted, there are a host of factors like your credit rating, property value, scale of investment, and their terms and environments that push the pins but hitting up the bank for a loan is pretty much ingrained in people's concepts of finance.

Oh, and remember to keep taxes kicking in there too. Your taxes generally constitute property tax, property insurance, mortgage insurance and homeowner association dues.

Private Lenders

Next up are private lenders. Basically, someone who isn't involved in commercial lending, like family or friends loaning you the money. Pretty easy to understand, right? Key here is typically striking an agreement that satisfies both the parties. These loans can really come in handy particularly if you're starting off, you don't have such a strict environment like banks, makes things exceptionally easier for everyone while you further grow your business.

Beware though, treat such loans the same as you'd do with loans from a bank. Not sorting out everything black and white properly upfront is a silly beginner's leak that breeds squabbles later on. The ole mix dough and friendship and you're bound to lose one mold is just too real to ignore this; do avoid handling anything verbally and sketch out an agreement that works with payments with everyone onboard with it!

Real Estate Partnerships

Remember the old saying two heads are better than one? Well, in real estate, two wallets are typically better than one. Setting up a real estate partnership lets you pool resources together by uniting forces with other investors to pull a rental property.

See why it's beneficial? Let's say to buy a rental property, we require $150K. If three people, me, you and Freddy get together, that's a mere $50K each. Add to that something brewing up and we three handle it together, sharing risks, profits while utilizing our strengths.

It's creating a legal partnership that everybody's agreed upon with specific roles, responsibilities, profits, losses all crisp chalked out for everyone to judge. Keep things clear, friend so you safeguard later down the line.

However, one disadvantage with real estate partnerships can be that legally all partners are considered personally liable for all debts and legal issues tied with the property — even if it was unrelated to their own conduct or investment. With this in mind, in the absence of a proper strong binding conditioned agreement, tread with caution.

Mortgage Loans

Mortgage Loans – A Reliable Financing Companion

Often viewed as the most reliable means of funding, mortgage loans have helped countless investors complete their rental property acquisitions. A mortgage loan describes a loan borrowed against real property, usually done with the assistance of a bank or specialized mortgage lenders. In such propositions, the filer agrees to repay their borrowed sum (including accruing interest) over a pre-determined time.

What sets mortgage loans apart from usual consumer or personal loans involves the usage of property as collateral within the agreement terms. In terminology terms, these borrowed funds come under the term asset-backed or collateral-based loans, ensuring banks earn regular payments or take control of real estate property as per loan terms.

Expectations on Down Payments

When obtaining the financing for rental properties, expect an initial down payment. Lenders seek security – evidence that filers intend to answer repayment periods genuinely. The down payment symbolizes the investor's financial commitment to the property. What you down pay any amount directly conditions the remaining loan balance.

Truthfully, an aspiring rental property owner must cover at least 20% of the property purchase price upfront–easing loan providers' mind since this portion psychologically assures a greater likelihood of the loan being recouped. Noticeably, this down payment rate rests higher than that needed for owner-occupied residential properties due to the increased risk carried by financing rental investments.

Variation of Mortgage Rates

Why do these down payments and interest rates remain higher than a standard home mortgage? Well, the answer resides within walls of risk. Lenders perceive rental property as prone to the risk of default – crossing paths both residential property mortgage and investor loans, this risk incentivizes higher mortgage fees. Noticeably, numerous factors decide mortgage rates applicable on rental properties. Key influencers pivot around credit score health, whereby those bolstering impeccable credit repertoires might enjoy access to low mortgage rates. Contrastingly, venturing investors with weak credit face substantial mortgage fees.

Drawbacks of Mortgage Loans

Full-scale awareness requires outlining pitfalls accompanying mortgage financing. Risk of foreclosures walks hand in hand with key challenges confronting passive income enthusiasts investing in rental income propensities. Foreclosure represents the process where lenders usurp properties if borrowers fail in fulfilling their loan obligations. Not only can such endings result in significant loss and damage one's credit, but resist efforts for future property investments.

Luckily, there's a silver lining to wary foreclosures – discipline in payments, i.e., denying procrastination a seat on the table, guarantees clean relationships between lenders and investors.

Practical Guidelines

Jumping further into acquiring mortgage-based investments dive heads in below points,

Do Your Homework: Understanding the pools swirling around mortgage rates practices augments financial literacy – enabling clientele drawing valuations and profiling their property investments through diverse mortgage loan perspectives.

Clarify Finances: Clear documentation over the financial situation bolster approval chances. Lenders significantly value financial stability, earning records, credit scores, and asset lists prior before diving in.

Hunt for Lenders: Cast your net of possibilities wide: traditional lenders doing loan unions, instructive banks, or specialized mortgage backgrounds draw powerful investment plans.

Do the Allegorical Math: Ignite calculating mindsets based on your chosen property. Master the mortgage, incorporate maintenance costs, accountant property manager fees or vacancies, to tug in profit.

Home Equity Loans

So... What's a Home Equity Loan?

Let's start with some basic understanding, shall we? Think of a home equity loan as your home's way of saying, "Hey buddy, you need money? Let's check how much you've paid off and see how I can help!" Essentially, a home equity loan allows homeowners to borrow against the equity they've built up in their primary residence. Now, by 'equity,' I mean the difference between the market value of your house and how much mortgage you still owe on it.

Think of your home as a piggy bank. As you make mortgage payment after mortgage payment, your piggy bank fills up with 'equity' pennies. if at some point you need some extra cash to make a bold real estate investment, you just need to rattle this piggy bank, your home's accumulated equity, give it a little shake, and voila! This approach is precisely what home equity loans offer. They're a particularly handy tool when considering rental properties or any major investment requiring sizable upfront capital.

You Pay Once, You Borrow Twice

One quirky thing about home equity loans is a feature often referred to as 'second mortgages.' Yes, you've heard it right. It might not be helpful if you're sick of paying your first one, but trust me; it's not as frightening as some people may paint it! Despite being called a second mortgage, this huge, scary phrase simply means you're re-borrowing money you were initially loaned to purchase your house. Pretty cheeky, right?

You might be wondering, "Why should I appreciate a second mortgage?" Let me tell you straight away that one critical advantage of a home equity loan is it usually carries a lower interest rate than other borrowing options, particularly unsecured ones. In simpler terms, it can get you the capital you need at a lesser coast! Plus, payments on home equity loans tend to be tax-deductible, adding sugar to the entire deal.

Understanding the Waves of Home Equity Loans

Like any good beach, home equity loans come with their own ebbs and flows in the plethora of choices they offer. These break down into two major types: standard home equity loans and home equity lines of credit.

Standard home equity loans, also known as term loans, are reminiscent of their mortgage cousins. You borrow the money upfront (keeping the equity right this time), repay it over an agreed term through fixed, equal monthly installments, walking you peacefully into a fully predictable repayment plan. Quite perfect if planning is your thing, my friend!

Diving into the potential second option, home equity lines of credit (HELOCs) are like your credit card, offering flexibility. Instead of borrowing a lump sum all at once, you can borrow as much as you need whenever you wish (within the limit of your established credit line). You only pay the interest for the utilized part, blending the maximum adaptability to match all your irregular borrowing needs.

As appealing as both might seem, stay cautious. Nothing should fit all unless spoken in the spirit of 'one size fits all - disaster,' might I add!

Couldn't Be Any Better Right, Wait, But What's That Closure Point?

Nothing is ever perfect my friend! Echoing this bitter-sweet life truth, using a home equity loan to finance your rental property also wields a double-edged sword. Go overboard, and you put your primary residence at risk. Essentially, should you default on this 'second mortgage,' you could face foreclosure and stumble into losing your house.

That's the reason to make sure you evaluate this financing route for all it's worth very strategically. Consider your risk tolerance, overall leverage, your potential income from the rental verse the loan repayment, and the current interest rates. Use your judgment, consult finance advisers or seek banking expertise before 'shaking your equity piggybank.'

Owner Financing

Let's imagine this scenario: You stumble across someone who
wants to sell their property like yesterday. Possibly, they might
have moved overseas, maybe going through a divorce, or things
are not too rosy financially. So, they want to sell it quickly. But,
guess what? Traditional lender ain't fast enough. So, what's the
solution? Enter Owner Financing.

In owner financing, instead of getting a loan from the bank, you'd
be getting a loan from the owner selling the property. More fun is,
your terms would be way more flexible since you ain't dealing
with a stuffed-shirt banker. Try asking for extra 30 days to repay
your bank loan and the reaction might send you scampering for
your cherished booze. But with the property owner, you're dealing
human-to-human—it's cooler and friendlier.

However, ask for all necessary ownership docs, because you
wouldn't want to bring your pyjamas sleaze-twirling cousin in-law
along while buying socks—in this case, bad property history.
Get it?

Private Investors

Here's the kicker! What if you don't like the idea of borrowing
money from banks (who does, they got too many dang rules—
sheesh!) or the property owner throws a curveball mumbling 'no
owner financing'. What do you do?

In such tight spots, you rise like a phoenix and look to the
infamous Private Investors. Now, these amazing people could be
individuals or companies hungrily on the wait to dish out cash in
exchange for a stake or an interest rate. In fact, sometimes, you
find private investors who've also been involved in property
renting themselves—the edge? They know the ropes, the yes-no,
the maybes and don'ts better than your Mother know how to get
your favourite shirt wrong, bless her heart!

However, before you become a bedfellow with private investors
you've got to learn the game—you enter like a novice, you could
fail miserably. Understanding your profit projections, carrying out
risk assessments or even providing enticing tax benefits are things
that get the seasoned private investors interested. If you can build
up this skill base, who bloody needs banks!

Crowdfunding

Remember those moments when you've with your mates,
plastered on the couch and enthralled like grinning possums
watching Shark Tank or Dragon Den? Businesses making

proposals and they would pool funds to finance them—that, my friend is what we call crowdfunding.

Some super smart folks thought to chisel this into the rental property realm too—crowdfunding property platforms. Say What? Dead right, mate! You and loads of other investors could pop money into a deal through a crowdfunding property platform—you get loads of credit and interest getting hands on heaps of greens—you're talking big league play.

As long as you're gambling with finances you're ballsy enough to lose-and account for tax liabilities, crowdfunding may get you covered. Remember, the pool reflects different egos and if the campaign ain't a knockout, some homeboys might want out early sure to shake things.

Hard Money Loans

Hard-Money Loans – Your Unique Avenue to Invest in Rental Properties

Why Hard Money Loans though? It should not surprise you if I said obtaining loans for rental properties is more challenging than procuring loans for a residential property – "challenging" always excites you, right? Especially financing could be no walk in the park if you are eager on duplexes, single-family rental homes, multi-family units, and all that exciting stuff. So typically, the lenders incline towards home loans as rental property loans are somewhat riskier from their view.

During your investment journey in the rental property market, you may reach a point when conventional housing loans products just won't cut the deal for you. Housing market fluctuations or strict credit requirements can furthermore make it tougher to secure these loans. At such times, looking beyond traditional financing would be wise. This is where hard money loans get a cue - as a fabulous opportunity for financing your awe-inspiring rental property pursuit!

What exactly are Hard Money Loans?

Here's what goes around in the streets… Hard Money loans are essentially short-term loans that real estate investors frequently use. It emphasises not much on you, dear borrower, but on the subject property's after repair 'value' and the fund itself is mostly given by private individuals, or say, private businesses unlike conventional lenders such as credit unions and banks.

Most bank loans have detailed and pretty ardent backgrounds and credit checks but Hard Money loans? They've got you covered!

They consider your credit a tad less. Who you are? Past records? Kidding me? Check your fico scores hahaha…just bring on a fabulous rental property for investment significance, a great venture, and Poe's Law – the doors to financing swings wide open, my friend!

The Handy Aspects

In our series of financing options for rental real estate investing, primarily Hard Money loans ought to be considered because of two things: One, these types of loans could hit your bank swifter, typically, within a few days or a week or so, when compared with traditional loans which could take weeks to materialize, maybe!

Speed is the need of the hour, isn't it?

Two – For real estate rehab scenarios or quick purchases where traditional lenders tend to retract their willing steps, landlords could easily rely on the untraditional – Hard Money loans. This is pretty much a problem-cracker in temporary financing, or as is the trendy word, bridge financing – especially if auction properties spark your interest.

Facing What's Hard

However, it's not all whisky and cigars. As it usually deals with distressed properties or high-risk deals - the catches that lure you - the risk, my friend, often outweighs the benefits! Sharp interest rates as compared to traditional forms of housing loans can be undoubtedly taxing. Additional loan origination fees, closing costs, or even prepayment penalties could be marked on your list!

Thus these kind of loans should be seen with the context of tentative real estate relationships and not long-term relationships. Lamentably compromising in regular rental income and possibly ending up in a default payment situation would not be music to any landlord's ears.

Moreover, as hard money lenders majorly concentrate on after repair value and recovery of the loan itself, rather than the borrower repayment capability, there is most of the time a lack of consumer protection. Hence treading this prudentially-oriented insurance-poor road, tread with your keen pair of eyes open for potential dangers or losses.

Investing 'Responsibly' With Hard-Money Loans

Despite having some cold shower realisations, if you still wish to flirt with the excitement that is rental property investments and Hard Money Loans; be prepared, harden your helm. As every investment strategy goes, prepare for unplanned scenarios such as potential vacancy periods, on-going maintenance or repair costs etc. Ensure sufficient cash reserves to avoid wrathful ticking off monthly repayments. Consider potential risks, cross-scenarios analysis, unseen costs remembering that while high risks reap high returns, they could also stick you hard.

A prudent pair of investors always reserve backing out as their viable ace card in the finance arena! And stick a flag on reliable findings from local experts, potential average rents estimates, doing your numbers correctly before leaping big!!

Keep an alt-tab close to speedy and famed rental property refinance lenders when you want to swap – Ever green outfits like Cash-out refinances could be your football-field across the elephantine bogs of sharp-interest ridden Hard Money loans!

A boring old story or not, experience is the sage. Practise due diligence, network with local real estate investors tinkering with so-called hard fortunes, find yourselves experienced A-rated Hard Money lenders – key essence of recipe untold, to die for.

In terms of financing options to invest in rental properties, hard money loans can be an attractive, non-traditional route - yet by the same token, it carries its share of challenges and risks. Use this information I shunned some early-evening light upon to propel you "swiftly" in making a shrewd leap.

Private Money Lenders

Who are Private Money Lenders?

Private Money Lenders (PMLs), my friend, are not corporate moguls. More often than not, they are individuals or groups with a substantial amount of cash looking to 'invest' their money for a return. Basically, they're someone you know or someone in your community, who's got plenty of dough, and is willing to offer a loan to you, typically at a much higher interest rate than the banks. naturally.

Pitching with Prowess

Now let me tell you…getting loans from PML does not involve any bureaucratic red tape, as you know, but the pivotal factor here is your relationship with them. It's based on collective faith as there may not always be a binding contractual agreement per se. So, here's rule numero uno - trust and reputation building are a little more than crucial. Yeah, I know, easier said than done, right?

So here's some tips on making it happen…A good pitch will swing things to your favor. Brief them crystal clear on why you're pursuing property finance with detailed specifics such as the type of property or local demographic drives. Chucking a quick but deep market research will light the whole deal on fire. Sweet, huh?

Interest Rates Madness

So, here's a friendly warning; they're not giving up their treasure for peanuts! Interest rates run way higher than bank loans varying between 10-15%, or even higher. Sure, it's pricy, but you got to do what you got to do, right?

Why the high prices? It's all about uniqueness, my friend. Traditional lending institutions requires substantial paperwork. With a private lender, things might not be that complicated. For example, in cases marked by hazardous conditions, quick payments are a blessing, although it is a good idea to have legal advice nearby to safeguard all transactions.

Risk Metrics & Mitigations

When getting caught in the 'Private Money Lenders'' radar, take note that they typically prefer a first trust deed with risk it carries. I mean, the lower the Loan to Value (LTV) ratio (the percentage of the home you're about to bankroll, to the total market price), the better for them as in the event of a default, foreclosure recovery is always pleasing favoring a lower ratio.

Gotta protect their backs, ya know?

Of course, solid equity creates reduced risks as theoretically, your costs could be covered by liquidating if worst came to worst. Taking that into consideration, you 'gotta have an optimum exit strategy handy too. Some satisfying scenarios to investors could be good credit history, previous flip profits, or even sweet success with a previous private money loan.

Jazz Mixed with Caution

As much as these private money lenders might be music to your ears (err pockets), proceed with caution my friend.

Why should you be cautious? Well, the rapacious interest rates, for one. And most importantly, transparency isn't too common amongst private money lenders. Though not bent on tricking people, the added mileage for them in money deals makes it easier for them to cut corners.

Whether it be predatory terms or exorbitant late fees, you've really gotta tread lightly with these guys. Also, exploring refinancing options (should you want out) or considering working jointly with another beginner investor could dampen the potential downfall before it ramps up too high.

What the Heck is Crowdfunding?

Well, bud, 'Crowdfunding is a method to raise funds (ka-ching!) from a large trove of investors who pool together their money to support a common project or cause'. This puppy of a concept offers limitless possibilities in an assortment of industries and is fast becoming the 'go-to' modus operandi for aspiring wanderers on the road to affording a rental property. Rent-rent-rent every paycheck away no more, jubilantly conjure your very own rental property business (how kickass does that sound?).

And guess what? There's such a smorgasbord of online crowdfunding platforms there, you'll swoon!

Network, marinate and invest with gazillions of like-minded folks hungrily hunting for a nifty way to finance their rental properties dreams. All this magic bestowed upon ye all from the comfort of your throne (the couch, really, where popcorn showers sonorously befall), with your dueling swords — a laptop plus a secured, virtual doorway called 'the internet'.

Pow! Bang! Boom! Falling dominos will line your way to purchasing your dear ol' house available for rent now.

How the Heck Does it Work Though, for Rental Properties?

I won't kid you, pal. Real estate crowdfunding isn't child's play but worry not! It isn't as labyrinthine a monster maze of meanness as one might imagine either.

Eager beavers climb aboard the crowdfunding train where they are, usually conveniently, cordoned off into segments — people who own a property, looking for investors (property parties), vs people sniffing diligently for grinding gears of the investment monster (money gents).

Party prop patrols maneuver through the countryside. Eyes narrowed, ears sharply tuned to rent-yielding opportunities — properties that have delectably rent-friendly prospects. They hunt, forage, catch one! Bringing it online, posting the project daredevil details to lure in, lo and behold, the monetary magi.

High priestesses and pontiffs of prospect probing are the crowdfunding middle-chiefs, leisurely scaling prospective projects that make the investing cut and whoosh…into the gladiatorial grounds they are flaunted. To the highest, freest bidders and bidet-using!

Money moguls, ship-jumping investors, save-ins-bloks Jacks and Jills ready for some bruising money-wrestling stake their belongings. They invest in the private, up & pronto property, tailor their bids to tango-down some expected returns, pore over humble-peregrines cap tables, split among fee waiting-lines, reap profits down the Sun-faced horizon life boulevard. Now ain't that a song and dance! ;)

Sounds pretty Out-Of-The-Box BoxOffice, doesn't it dude? What Say Example-ya?

Imagine you set sail on an exotic treasure hunt (been addicted to pirate visual of late, humor the old man). You learn of a sizzling property pulsating potent profits, price peaking at, let's say, 100 precious doubloons. Ain't none of your pockets horsing around these unicorns. Drats!

Man, the decks, throw the SOS tube online within crowdfunding waters. Fellow raft captains cataloguing a domino tally of 1 doubloon each might express interest — treasure hunters look out for fellow skin!

Money magic multiplication commences, amassing the required booty for the winnings fair. With the enigmatic key secured, you purchase Xanadu. The players bearing their lone doubloon-sticks, monetarily invested victors, have opened a mighty Pandora's box of rental profit-sharing goodness.

Chapter 5: Finding and Evaluating Properties

Effective Property Search Strategies

Let's talk about finding and properly evaluating properties. Whether you're looking to buy your forever home, make an investment or find the right space for your business, these strategies can prove most effective.

1. Detail Your Property "Wishlist"

Let's start off by answering a basic question. What do you want from the property you're on the lookout for? Finding the answer to this question will help you streamline your search (and believe me, between those online classifieds and agency websites, you'll want your search to be as efficient as possible).

For instance, you will want to note the type of property – condo, commercial space, building lot and so forth. Don't forget about location – you know what they say about real estate - location, location, location. Should it be close to the city centre or a particular market? Outline other key factors, like price range, desired vicinity, and housing style to customize the search. Be thorough with the list, and importantly, keep yourself from pressing "Request Information" on every nice-looking property on the web!

2. Use Multiple Channels for Your Search

Unlike 20 years ago, getting hold of properties now doesn't ALWAYS involve a real estate agent. Technology and digitalization have got your back. Nowadays we have property websites offering homes, flats or whatever it is you prefer. This has brought down locational barriers and now you can view properties nationwide within a matter of minutes without leaving your couch. Factor in social media outlets such as Facebook's marketplace or property-specific Facebook groups and you're walking into a supermarket of properties. So, explore all these avenues, keep your eyes open and who knows you might just stumble into a golden find.

3. Get a Real Estate Agent Involved

Now having said all that, let's not disregard the charm of a conventional real estate agent. Sometimes, old school is cool. Local seasoned property agents can have access to information and deals that aren't up on the web. The guidance they provide is undeniably advantageous: they're cognizant about the market conditions, pricing, and negotiation dynamics; foremost, they understand legality like the back of their hand. Collaborating with an agent can, in fact, aid you to avoid potentially risky blunders.

4. Conduct an In-Depth Property Evaluation

So you've found a few properties that met your noted criteria and are in your price range. Well done! However, next comes an even more important step: an in-depth evaluation.

Due Diligence - This part, my friend, is crucial to your endgame. First, you need to do a thorough physical check of the building, often categorized as a "structural survey. Evaluate the structural strength, electrical and plumbing systems, air conditioning, and heating system - any potential issues that could cost you in the long term. Finding and understanding the total operations cost of a building can likewise be instrumental towards successful property acquisition.

Inspect the legality and regulatory details of the property meticulously. Review the documents very carefully since they determine property rights, condition background and entitlements. All these details are key-pieces that form the full picture of the property under consideration.

Be prudent, be thorough – do not rush. Hasten slowly but properly weigh property's exteriors and interiors – compare this assessment with your wish list. Remember they are indicators not only immediate expenditures but also of future potential costs.

5. Negotiate Like a Boss

If you're like me, then honestly, negotiating is an uncomfortable task. But, regardless, here is a powerful mantra you must own: everything is negotiable. The asking price for a property may well not always represent the bottom-line. Borrowing from Kenny Rogers' wisdom, "You've got to know when to hold 'em". Negotiation is a fine art it's all about understanding psychological behavior of the party across the table. Play same game they could play, don't verbalize an exact amount, rather set it between the margin – it's all about the mighty little chat.

And there you are with your effective search and evaluation strategies, ready to go on your property-finding journey. It might be one full of hunting, evaluating and lots of negotiating, sure. But, remember — it could ultimately lead you to your dream home or yield a significant return on your entrepreneurial architecture. So it is about taking both the strides and stride out intelligently coupled with determination!

When it comes to property investment, picking a property is not just a random choice, there is art and some science to be mastered in evaluating a property's potential and determining if it's just giving a facade of profit magnet, or if it indeed carries the return on investment charm. As the saying goes, all that shines isn't necessarily gold. Hold onto your hard hat and drill beyond the paint, pin down the property puzzle pieces! Buckle up!
Let's dive in.

An Insider Glance - Property Condition

The condition of a property plays a pivotal role when investing. A sparkling, spick and span property tempts you right away, doesn't it? But let that emotion go, think rationally. It's not just about how it looks, but also how fit it is really from within. Yes, the heart should beat fine, as in, the basic infrastructure, critical specifications like plumbing and wiring to name a few.

Upon sketchy surface, many properties allure you with luscious lawns and aesthetic appeal, but the hidden horrors might just sham those fascinating firsts. Here, appoint a professional inspector, builders, or handymen that align with your intentions can save you a fortune in the longer haul and flag the unwanted surprises. Overall, always remember no matter how tempted, elevated, or enamored you feel, your eye should twinkle only at 'potential properties' and careful inspection followed by thorough scrutiny should be the winning trump card.

Picture 'Potential' and Plot Profit

The 'P square' or picture a profit and analyze it by bringing in basic metrics, statistical models, and industry insights on the table. Profit is your shrine here, all roads in the property investment space should lead to profit. This could be achieved differently for each individual investor. For instance, Andy might be all in for office properties for flashy returns whilst Sally may smirk at the stability in residential property rents. So, the P square differs, and meticulously must be modeled into your overall strategy.

Also, potential envisages not just the 'who?' as in types of properties you see potential in, but 'where?' is equally commanding too. Remember location, location, and location? Never shy away to push the mapping compass a tad more agilely while identifying and elevating potential based on a targeted location. Connect the neighborhood schools, offices, hospitals, transport hubs, all the scenes in the vicinity. With real estate investment there isn't a one-size-fits-all strategy, however having detailed metrics and probability on your side gives a stake on approaching calculated risks.

Keep Calm and Choose the Right Neighborhood

You may have found the perfect house – spacious, bright, open-concept kitchen (just like we all see on those cooking shows), but have you ever thought about the community atmosphere? These are all important aspects of a property, but I can't emphasize enough: LOCATION IS EVERYTHING, dude!

Bear in mind, you can change your property, but you can't relocate an entire neighbourhood. Undeniably, the house to purchase does matter, but it's the choice of your neighbourhood which plays a greater role in dictating the quality of your life for years, even decades, to come.

Key Points When Checking Out the 'Hood

When you're looking at lovely houses and imagining them as your dream home, it's simple to get smitten by a striking characteristic or upgrades. However, you need to always remind yourself to thoroughly evaluate the overall surroundings. They should perfectly match, or at least complement, your way of life. Don't know where to start? Here are four words: Safety. Accessibility. Appeal. Future.

Safety: Unless all you care about is the thrill of living in a 'live or die' neighbourhood (which I'm pretty sure isn't the case), check out the crime rates, neighbourhood watches, presence of authority and all the related safety details. A couple of appropriate questions to ask may include, people leaving their doors open or a history of break-ins.

Accessibility : Let's talk logistics. Think about your daily life. How easy would it be for you to get to work? What about hitting up the gym or the grocery market? Where's the nearest hospital? Remember, traffic and transportation services can make getting to and from a place better – or worse.

Appeal : Does the neighbourhood appeal to you? Check out parks, clean streets, friendly locals, and well-maintained homes. You got to have feel-good vibes, pal!

Future : Part of evaluating a property includes considering its future potential. Be that savvy bloke who's not just thinking about your next 5 years, but someone investing in their long-haul journey.

Essential Amenities to Count On

Just as how asking for free wi-fi upon checking in your resort is important, considering amenities is crucial too. It's those extras that enhance the overall quality of the place. To kick things off, here are some basic ones that everyone generally expects: easy access to shopping, schools, restaurants, public transportation, parks, and even those morning cafes!

Do you love sweating out in spin classes, washing down your awkward dance moves with expensive IPA or maybe just swinging hula-hoops on open-air fests? Intricately plan how much these daily luxuries matter when choosing your new neighbourhood, and in evaluating properties.

If living in an exclusive suburban comfortably sipping on Pinot Noir amid garden-zested mood lights subjects your being to frisson, look out for posh wine and dine places, and carefully landscaped public spaces. Check in with hoity-toity folks possibly to be your neighbours (or not).

The bottom-line, though, my friend, is being granted the privilege to live in a premium comfort so remember to have a wholesome checklist catering to the 'You' - both what it's today and what it may morph into future.

Shouting out the cliché: A well begun is HALF done - man, you're in for a pretty productive journey. Yes, this task of assessing neighborhood and looking up the amenities while both agitating and exciting, gives you astonishing power plus supremacy. Indeed, it does. Tiny bits stacked upon one another to build lifetime galleries.

Finally, it's necessary to comprehend that the very benefit of the great location—providences to amenities, bustling economy, and venerable schools—proposes that property values and taxes might surely be higher too but well, money is just a thing eh?

Calculating Potential Returns and Cash Flow

The Search for Property Returns Gold!

Remember that yard where buried treasures or sea of diamonds in fairy tales come from? Finding an investment property is kind of like that! However, in real estate, the lushly returns aren't stashed in a genie's magic lantern. Rather, the lucre truly lies within the property's potential to generate a continual income stream or cash flow.

With me until now? Alright! Let's move on.

So, How Do I Scavenge Nuggets of Cash Returns?

In a way, lucrative properties functionally like a groovy little goose tirelessly laying all these golden eggs called financial gain except gold nowadays is a hairy real-life equation called ROI or Return on Investment.

So, if your Real Estate Hogwarts letter somehow feigned a delivery mishap (Ouch, that smarts, right?), make yourself comfortable as we glide through this muggle version of the magical journey to un-riddle the ROI math.

De-Mucking the Return on Investment!

ROI encapsulates all potential profits returned on the amount invested in a property. Familiarizing with it helps you skim off undesired prospects to zero in on more potential profit-bearing properties.

Let's dive into simplified stages of this calculation. First, submerge the original investment cost from the eventual earnings. Then, divide that result by the original investment and, finally, shazam— you reach an ecclesiastical gold-mine of ROI percentage!

Comfortable with the concept already? Let's develop this further with, umm... say we just acquired an irresistible granny flat for $120,000 and assuming eight years later it attributes a scrap of $240,000. That is, the total return will stand - placeholder at eight years - as: $(240,000 - 120,000)/120,000 \times 100\% = 100\%$. An exciting double of our purchase cost sounds like a juicy pick— doesn't it?

Now, Let's Jingle Those Coins: Calculating Cash Flow!

Enjoyed 'treasure-hunting' so far? Well, cranking cash flow deciphering gears will equally bubble excitement—enough to make Scrooge McDuck flinch in awe! Cash flow equates the net earnings or losses from the property each year, a significant pointer towards your earning capacity via the investment.

Peek behind the cash flow curtains mirrors, gross income - overheads, including mortgage repayments, insurance costs, property taxes, among others gripping the finery of your furrowed billionaire brow. So, hand me the leisure of math-ing it up as: Cash flow = Gross year income - Operational expenditures.

Yes, Cash Flow Turns Green and Red!

A green flow states earning profits where the maintenance and arrears rendered the monthly rent or lease—and positively so. Conversely, a negative flow hemorrhages your pockets, throwing you in direct headlights of a costlier property than initially perceived.

Before we potter back to our regular lives un-Scrooged before, remember a positive cash flow isn't the be-all and end-all. At times, taking a long-term view of an appreciating negative scoring deal can yield wildly high results within the right investment palette.

But enough about muggles' numerology! You now possess a quill-touch away from trans mapping obscure real estate properties into legible business reputes founded on understanding ROI calculations and Cash Flow.

Squint no more at unknown property prospects but venture smashing calculated financial foresight. You'll soon strut off glass gleam floors—tan all powdered by abundant treasure sunbathed, clarifying investments paired effortlessly clutching strings to tighten lucrative ownership ropes.

Chapter 6: Acquiring Rental Properties

Negotiating Purchase Agreements

Be ready, negotiating purchase agreements for rental properties might look arduous and stressful at first glance. But trust me, it's more mathematic than magic, more about being slicker than your average and wouldn't it be wise to bear some enlightened perspectives both based from my knowledge, research and invaluable experience. So, staph yourselves, so much to peel back.

Leverage Information

It's like heading to the battle field, right? Well how about knowing where you stand? That's just prepping, and a crucial key aspect nonetheless is doing a ton of research, forever upfront. You're going to want to research the property's history thoroughly. Things like fair market value, the neighborhood, age of the building, knowing if risk amendments (like environmental problems, degradation, pest invasion, fires and if it's ever been prey to seasonal natural disasters) have added costs to it, understanding how long it's been in the market or if there had been frequent ownership changes.

These can inform you about the property's physical and legislative conditions, position your dear & near data reservoir that probably can translate to sources revealing if the seller is desperate to sell immediately for fast shell shock cash or they mightn't be care and can wait.

Think Creatively

Remember it's not always the best price that wins. Here's the mindset, imagine the unimaginable son! Big Picture Fanatic, something close-to Einstein's out-of-the-box thinking - You studying Abstract Art yeah?

It's true some sellers might cash it immediately, but others could wait, for, let's say – someone who can maintain, safeguard probably like the proverbial story of a pearl in the oyster or mayn't refrain but have created sentimental connection with a property not just to anyone but ensuring the legacy resonate.

So, when sweetening the deal, besides a beneficial offer, try including things you're willing to address: carry costs for a certain period, clean out any debris remaining on property upon transfer and more.

Tailored letters can lead to great thing and one enclosing why the property you're trying to close is of significance to you could light that spark. Who knows sharing why you love the garden behind the property could light seller's sentimental value besides monetary figures? Seen that happening! Enlightening, isn't it?

Well Crafted Contingencies

Reeling someone with high bait and picking the heat off just isn't realistic. Abide by the Bible – you re-negotiate here, it'll come back nibbling at you at some point enroute. In pain, terms like financing, _inspecting + appraising the property as well as closure timescale can bell this tortuous cat. Hence securing contract creation to help stall after initial vibe perusal – No one here is a master stroker!

What they do is give you explicit time for deep research - financer re-eligibility sequences, realizing property's winning scale taking into, say intricate marketing research perspectives change and 'course crucial sale points that enables higher perusal time from real estate syndication regulations etymology.

Now it's game on!

Honest and Frank Discussions

Ideally, all contractual agreements wrap up nice'ly like newly crocheted quilt and timely run-of-the-mill weekly reading list subscribed back right on. What about both side breaches like if time load's severed improperly or in cases like earnest transactions fail?

Fact is there would be consequences to play by, potentially leading to contract terminations and - fiscal or socially draining - face-offs. Therefore, building truthful, honest and effective communication layer is the art here. Flexibility will be cherished where interests are protected but each have their cards played in a win-win manifested podium.

Keeping your Emotions in Check

Negotiating really exciting can – messes you, emotions running ahead without harness, go carefully my friend. Never allow your behavioral tone, sign bearing upset antics infiltrate your deal cracking strategy. Multiple pro-window open would necessarily provide elegantly onto alternate landing points - the wild card. Spread thin – butter 'n bread. Understand, probably clearer every next pro-floor clean-up pitched solution stick timely.

<u>Due Diligence – Making Property Decisions Worth Your While</u>
So, due diligence... Sounds serious, doesn't it? It sure is! At its simplest, due diligence, in the context of acquiring rental properties, is an all-round investigation or audit into a potential investment opportunity. By carrying out due diligence, you equip yourself with every last pore of information - a way of ensuring that you don't get snagged shock-spiked. Plus, you keep your wallet safe from bad deals!

Conventional due diligence process
Here's a walkthrough of a typical due diligence process. Remember, the steps may vary a smidge depending on the nature of the property; however, generally this should give you an overarching understanding.

1. Financial analysis: Before an inspection takes place or attending an open viewing, it is crucial to be satisfied with numbers. Evaluate rental history, operational costs, property taxes, vacancy rates etc., and then define your key metrics like cap rate, ROI, cash on cash, or internal rate of return. Here's an even simpler tip: if maths makes you yawn and you're doubting the numbers, trust your gut and hold back on that offer instead of proceeding with the thumbs up.

2. Title search: A crucial part of due diligence is ensuring the property title is squeaky clean. Hiring a reputable title agency can work wonders for recognising any defects, liens, or easements tied to the deed that may potentially throw spanner in the works in the process of ownership transfer. This way, you don't end up holding the bag!

3. Regional study: Lastly, make sure the property is located in a stunning neighbourhood. Researching about traffic patterns, opportunities for development, the supply-demands gaps in rentals existing there, upcoming zoning plans, i.e., simply pulling out a macro lens on the area in which your potential rental exists can prove to be invaluable. Tools like Mashvisor, City-data can make the job so much easier.

Property Inspections – Don't Miss this Bite
Next up, it's all about property inspections. Sure, the house looked beautiful at first glance, the butterflies in your stomach giggling with joy. Heard of 'beauty is only skin-deep', eh? Unattended repairs or faults in construction can blow money and cause enough grey hair in the long run.

Why Do I Need A Property Inspection?

A professional property inspection gives a comprehensive overview of the status of their prospective buy: what works, what doesn't, what needs immediate attention and what might be a problem say two years down the line?

Different Types of Property Inspections

Your property inspection's scope and level of detail will vary depending on the type of inspection undertaken. Conventional inspections are as follows:

Structural inspection: Reviewing supporting components like the foundation, rooves, walls or beams for integrity.

Plumbing inspection: Check those leaking taps, discharge lines or nasty stuff drained improperly(bummer!)

Electrical inspection: To scout for outdated or faulty wiring that could pose health hazards.

HVAC inspection: To assess the functioning of the heating, ventilation, and cooling systems.

Environmental/damage inspection: Lastly, scout for hazardous materials, presence of mold, mildew, or damage by termites(yuck!)

Property Inspector Checklist

A property inspection is only worthwhile if it is conducted by a trusted and vastly experienced property inspector. Find an inspector who is competent enough to evaluate everything – from possible damp locations to home insulation, the backyards, the heating unit, roofing – all fundamental 'must-goes' in the checklist. Include larger, more expensive repair items so you can justify the final price you're ready to offer.

Alright, that must be quite the bunch to take in, right?

Closing the Deal and Legal Considerations

Closing the Deal

So, after finally finding the investment-worthy rental property, negotiating the right terms and securing the necessary finances to buy it, now what? Sure, it's time to officially close the deal. But how? Uh, it's not as simple as making the money transaction - 'whoosh' and Bam! – it's yours.

No, my friend, this is where you'll encounter the 'Closing' – an affectionate or not-so-affectionate term for the final negotiation process of a real-estate venture. It's the last serving of this scrumptious 'buying a property' soup where the legalities swoop in with a swish of more negotiations. Let's go one step at a time.

Step1: Preparing Closing Documents

Sounds bureaucratic and bland, but bear with me. The attorney or the title company you'd hire will prepare the settlement statement, specifying varying costs leviable and undertaken by you and the seller during the closing process.

Next on the menu - the Deed. The ownership flag that historically was handed over at the successful closure of deal in fairy tales – try imagine that! The Deed signifies transferring of the property to you, and is prepared by the attorney or title company.

Step2: A Final Review

Ahem! My wise friend, always aint it's better to read before you sign? Now's the day you officially pour all that profound wisdom in action. Before signing the papers, take your 'read it before signing it' mantra including a choir musical out in open.

Look at: Loan Documents, Property Insurance and, settlement Statement.

Seem complicated and daunting? Bring your mortgage advisor in the picture to look it all over with keen eyes.

Transference of ownership – The star moment!

Once those devilishly twirling details have been dealt with, move towards signing those exhausting official looking papers – to imprint your blessed name as the new owner! Ensure, double ensure that the 'grant of the deed' and 'rents & profits' all are transferred to you by the seller smoothly.

And so, my dear friend, you taste the mighty powers of being an official landlord! Voila! Add up another buddy to your profile entourage! - The Real Estate Owner!

Hail to this victory!
Legalities swooping in!

With power comes responsibility, right? Alongside, the challenging winding often confounding company of legalities associate & whisk along unannounced. So, here's a clue yet essential lowdown on the glow – at logical likely words trickling out of fathomless legal-jargon ocean!

The Land Property Act, Easements & Positive and Restrictive Covenants

Sounds like different planets with similar city specific logos stamped, huh? Well line dancing they are. These terms, though paradoxically your new best friends and unrelenting adversaries. Ostensibly hovering over territories masked as tenants-right-protection, they in reality cloak grey zones with a predisposition to spawn tangles in your carnival.

Easements , trooping in from Commons sphere, refers to rights sheltered with another party permitting bona fide use of your property!

Positive Covenants, sort of wizard waving wands casting you prescribed actions you must follow as the owner post possession. Restrictive Covenants, well the reverse cousins declaiming stark varnished rules that bind what you CAN'T do with your property.

Financing and Securing the Property

I know you've been doing some research lately about getting into the rental property game, and I wanted to talk to you a bit about financing and securing rental properties, one of the very key aspects of your adventurous real estate journey. This whole business venture can seem intimidating, but trust me, once you know what you're up to, it's totally manageable! So, let's dive in, shall we?

Deciding on the type of finance

The first thing you want to do when walking down the financing path is figuring out how much money you will need and the best way to acquire it. There are actually quite a few financing options available. Maybe you have something in mind, maybe you're not sure. I'll just summarize the main ones, so you can get a better overview.

Self-financing

If you've been quite the saver, you might just go ahead and self-finance the entire purchase. This is the most straightforward way, but of course, it is dependent on how much money you have saved up.

Traditional bank loans

Most of us will probably think about going over straight to a bank for a traditional mortgage. The interest rates on these loans have been pretty reasonable as of late, you have more or less regular payments, and it has worked for many, so why not? Make sure to check what you qualify for and get pre-approved!

Hard money loan

A less conventional option could be to use a hard money loan if you're pinched for time or need to stick out in this increasingly competitive real estate market - these loans have faster approval. However, remember the interest rates can be quite high, and terms and conditions quite harsh; are you really up for that?

Non-traditional loans

Going over to aunt Lucy to borrow some money? Well those

family loans can work out pretty well! It seems informal, but actually it does help to lay out a real loan contract with all the terms, to avoid ending up tossed out during your annual family barbecue. Yeah, Aunt Lucy values her returns pretty much…

Groundwork Needed for Securing a Loan

My main advice is don't rush the process – thorough preparation is key! First off, your credit score – how shiny is it? You'll need it spotless as it'll affect your interest rates. Ideally, you want to check this out about a year before proceeding with investing just so you can smoothen out any bumps.

Provide a proof of stable income next. They will also need things like W-2 statements, pay-check stubs for the past two years and, of course, your federal tax returns. Spending history and outstanding debts will be assessed to get an overview of your financial capabilities.

Being able to present a solid business plan can also sway your chances on your side. No, I don't mean that one sketched on a cocktail napkin! Put in all relevant financial details of the property, including estimated maintenance costs, projected rental income, etc.

Down Payments

Moving onto down payments! Probably everyone has it in mind that anything less than 20% down means you've to pay private mortgage insurance. That's an extra layer on top of the cake called your monthly pay-outs. So perhaps, try to scrap together that 20% figure; typical requirements, though, for investment properties could be even higher, around the 25-30% mark.
And coming to closing costs, these can be aplenty, from appraisal fees to mortgage applications and more – you might be from 2% to 5% out of your total price! Keep some room for these before you plunge into this pool.

Securing the Property

When everything is in order money-wise, you can start the closing process and think about securing your property. Your first big task is getting appropriate insurance. Landlords need more coverage than traditional homeowners, so this requires a specific landlord or rental property insurance policy. You're obliged to insure the structure of the building, but also the legal liability! We cannot shortcut this process.

Finally adding extra layers to your security could mean demanding appropriate security deposits and installing rental property securities like alarms or appropriate locks of doors and windows.

Just note, securing and financing your rental property isn't a sprint but a long-distance run. Put in the time into planning, control the controllable, and don't skimp on solid payment plans and securing the property. Race wisely and you'll be wakening yourself up earning money in your pajamas!

I hope getting through all these areas will help shield you against financial "surprises" further down the line! It might be heavy early on and maybe there's a whole lot more paperwork than casual chatter over a beer. But once it's done, rinsing and repeating is a whole lot easier, I promise!

Chapter 7: Property Management and Maintenance

Essential Property Management Tasks

Yes, my lovely friend! Today, our chit-chat revolves around property management, something that raises our eyebrows, but, trust me, it's as exciting as binge-watching your favorite series. So, cup of coffee (or tea!) by your side? Let's march into this riveting maze of bricks and bones of buildings.

7.1 - that may sound like a boring math problem you had once, but here it's the fulcrum to all our property management awe. Let's talk about what we face as property owners or hopeful future landlords. Surely, we frequently dread the tidal way of everyday tasks, don't we? If the site of your ever-piling unread emails and pending calls were triggering your Pandora's box of unrealized superstitious fear, my dear buddy, welcome to your invincibility cloak!

Essential Property Management Tasks

If I would ask you to draw an image representing Property management- it would probably display some checking-account-cheating utilities, rough-housed tenants, or mirage-creating building repair needs! Don't fret! These tasks are as manageable as your morning yoga routine. All depends on the discipline, consistency and yes, not compromising with Savasana, am I right? Conclusively, let's chat about those really, REALLY, well let's put it that way "indispensably" important tasks in property management.

Property Maintenance: Here's the first reality check -The Flat ain't no Fairytale Castle honey! So let's regroup our fantastical dreams into a responsible fist of fore-thought. Managing regular maintenance like plumbing or cooling & heating issues deliver two magical gifts – "Happy tenants" and "Blockage-protected" Longevity of your property!

Responding to Tenant Requests: Do we prefer those soggy nachos before a euphoric mid-night movie? Of course, not! Similarly, our good ol' tenants repel procrastination faced during their requested fulfilments. Responsiveness from landlords "boostify" the tenants' trust, quite like topping on nachos, and why not be a super heroic task completer! Every little thing kept right draws a long communal relationship, reflected in your echoing guest-rooms!

Regular Property Inspections: If morning walks swirl herbal

freshness to your start-of-the day dew, here's one wholesome ingredient to it! Regular check-ups hold the essence of successful management. You know it gives wings of vigour to your early-bird rises, isn't it?

Rent Collection: Tell me, how boring does the taste of your hazelnut-fruity Coffee become before an unsaid long wait? Yes! Sync your tenants' rent submission diligence with direct withdrawal EC mandates, giving that smooth voyage to your well-awaited bank showcase.

Accommodating Incoming & Outgoing Tenants: Love-watch Bird-box with all high-quality lachrymal movements during arrivals and heart-wrenching final goodbyes? Yeah, am painting the stark similarity to our tenants' first apparition vs pass-bys scheduled or non-scheduled. Maintain the move-in out inventories, check of past possessed tenant dues or key-safe hand-offs like quintessential science!

Vendor Relationship Management: Lightened up at the mention of Ice-cream, coffee, pizza vendors? Heck yeah! Make you joyful breeze tenants joy-cones just so whip creamed! Varied Site repair vendors your property pearl neck-piece management feathers aren't they?

Keeping Detailed Records: The day your favourite Novel marked another ended volume isn't a grim ending! Instead paved that sunrise gate for follow-up reads, doesn't it? So remember each tenant is a beautiful chapter creation in your mansion-volume epic living! Track transactional details like a timeless romantic story recollection, my truest buddies!

There are hats of many kinds to these iconic tasks. However, let us remember, what strikes perfection completeness not bone-free meth arms! So let's recollect all forms of property hope flags we laid. Property Maintenance, Tenant communication, Regular Property checks & Rent Collection aren't back-clenchers remember? Incoming- outgoing tenant responsibilities or custodianship isn't our single massive villain-oic faceoff! Fare-well negotiation handling or the much fascinating duty-based management records may burn the slow-talk candle miles down. Someone has truly spat poetically here, Perfecting is not timing perfectionist turns, aren't they? These rigid compiled task-mates lose to your "structured order-zoning". Why don't we celebrate these amazing realities all through our inherent property-"believing process" folks?

Firstly, let me tell you, at the core of successful property management and maintenance is, no surprise, a formidable tenant. You can't deny it; they literally compose the key piece of the puzzle. So, if we're down to brass tacks, one BAD tenant can bring monumental disaster - you snap your fingers and bang; there goes your sleep times and sanity while firefights potential property damage, rent issues and legal conundrums.

But hold on, there. Let's chill out. All it requires is figured out how to find and screen your future tenants, to win the rental game.

Why is Finding Reliable tenants So Crucial?

First, let's understand why real la crème de la crème tenant is a dream come true for any property owner. Proper occupants assure a constant cash flow through continuous and timely rental payments - it sorta flows like clockwork. They also take relative care of rental spaces, saving you from unnecessary repair and maintenance costs. Driving the tale home, reliable tenants are akin to silent caretakers - aiding the upkeep and increasing the property value. Simply put, they're like your property elves giving you peace of mind, making long-term rental a cakewalk. So buckle up, your buddy is here to show you the ropes of procuring reliable tenants.

How-to Grass-roots: Craft an Attractive Rental Ad

First and foremost, an attractive rental advertisement piques the interest from potential quality renters. Consider this: if your depiction of the property is duller than dishwater, or non-existent, brace yourself for similarly inclined occupants. On the contrary, showing the best attributes of your property through attractive descriptions and quality photos will inevitably attract prospective virtuoso tenants. Remember, we live in a digital world. Work it often and work it well!

Flex Those Sniper Scopes—Screening Prospective Tenants

Next door is how adequately you screen the prospects, starting down the central road of a rental application. Amidst other trivia stuff, collect details like their name, phone numbers, number of occupants, and of course, pet details because we all love them fur babies.

Expanding it to a basic trifecta, eye their financial stability, rental history, and character references. Validate their income proof and run a mandatory credit check—these details work well enough to cover the highlight reel of their monetary capabilities and habits.

You wouldn't want an evasive night dweller raising their fearful heads now, would you?

Unearthing possible dispossession judgments or bankruptcy may help too. It's not trophy stuff, but it warns you against occupants adept at the 'Free-Lodging Freeway Adventure'.

For the rental history, don't hesitate to communicate with previous landlords. Give them a jingle or a slight elbow tap. Their experiences and eagerness (or lack thereof) are tail-trailers and speak galactic tones about your applicant.

You and the Reservoir: The Laws and Anti-Discriminatory Policies

And, of course, understanding the Fair Housing Laws and Anti-discriminatory policies. Legal quagmires and your best sleep are immiscible fluids. Best follow up with this one. I mean you have to put your John Hancock plenty, but wincing over those legal documents actually bears considerable heft. Dodge discriminatory complaints and besides, it produces a positive spirit in retrospect towards your prospects.

The Art of Human Interactions: "The Interview"

Rounding up The Runaways, sit with your prospective occupant : oh, the informal yet-focused interview casts obvious-yet-unseen screening aspects. Carefully supervise how they carry themselves, the general realization, sprouting issues they currently have with their landlords—these hover in the Zone 66 of tedious nature but remember what we're eyeing here, right?

Chevys on bricks—The Agreement terms

Ultimately, cast out your precious capture net, a detailed yet sensible tenant agreement or lease terms. Natural Language just like this doesn't ooze out in them, but you better dish a lot. It must faithfully reflect terms on deposit variety, rental due date, property maintenance clause, sign on rent escalation and termination policies. But, don't relegate other potential benign-appearing classifications like rules on smoking, guest visitors and my fav, those wise fur-faced pet policies to never consulted realms. There's no throw-a-bone-to dynamics, but reviews carry lasting footprints after bold move-ins concluded, quite decisively. So you had your light hours shot chewing on views, sorting laws, odd conducts, hidden pitfalls, planning an interview styles, and setting out clauses. Those results—I can bet, will bring a rainbow round up with your new, reliable tenant making the sun shining for fulfilling property ownership and easy long-term friendship. Curiously, it did slug as dry-sliced for several compadres; yours included truly here. But oh boy! Show me one venture which doesn't reap fresh off life satisfaction as we pull off our determination spree.

A-la-recherche—dona thou recluses shake away any imagined weaknesses for proactive beings' chip robustly lively objectives. Unless one begins, where else are conclusively felt purposeful alignments found? Create joy. Completed phases help realise glimpses of amusing layers fallen reveal under the weight of contemplative success, warming to even gently-rattling chips frozen on frosty times.

Kick-off. Begin Property Rental Journey

Mark my blurt: make your tenants your friendly co-pilots in this rental journey. Saving all the peril of unpredictability where human traits flip realities, controlling aspects beforehand rarely flips peace in retrospect generally calling after piecemeal chunks of experiences lump colourful entropy. Nature drawn to recovery and drawn from generous chapters defining security either creates social composure, waiting rebounds of success for flutter invigilating reflections, leaving behind potential financial accomplishment.

So before signing dusky blues sentiments, this compelling dive-off results and effect: on-field experience is no hassle training. Read. Dig. Turn in and reflect on triggers before handling that magnet denoted due schedules—being rewarded essence accompanied by deeply-penetrative vibes. Come, oh beautiful shreds of defeat seeming the iceberg of Victory beneath a collective flake taking names, reminding quintessential stances.

Great tenants bless semi-crystal sentiments calming rides speaking sunshine. Long term solace describes ice on sultry Sunday morning between amicable conversation with kates and fluffy pillows enclosing brilliant themes and contemplating fulfilled breaks sliced by the edge of pristine culmination we terms—meaningful yonder unto future!

Lease Agreements and Rental Policies

Can we put aside our usual coffee talk about gadgets, automobiles, or lifestyle, to slipping into something critical and intriguing? It's all about 'lease agreements and rental policies' - a significant key not just to those in big shot-esque business investments sector but also to common people like us.

As you fill up on your caffeine needs, think about this: Ever thought how thousands of people across the country maintain their livelihood by giving out their properties for rent or as more people are moving across destinations for work or pleasure, there probably is a woven tapestry of laws and regulations that keeps all these dealings fair and lawful?

Let's flip some regular mindsets. Tonight, the beans we are going to spill are not the tales of conventional 'landlord-gone-bad' or 'tenants-from-hell.' Instead, we dive into some lesser-noticed waters – your lease paperwork and rental strategies.

Crowning Lease Agreements as King

Wait! Lease agreements and strategies have you anxious? Don't lack sleep over them, have another sip of your coffee, and Let's explain why putting your ears around this will only do you good. Writing (or should I say, righting?) a lease agreement can't be an eloquent process. Agreed. Yet, pal, can I tell you this hides the real essence - it's the backbone of a good rental partnership. This document sums up everything, from overdue fees to the rights and responsibilities of both tenant and landlord. Isn't it pretty much the Constitution of your property world?!

The principle we promote is perfectly encapsulated in Mahatma Gandhi's saying, "The future depends on what you do today."

A tiny bit labor by defining comprehensive leasing arrangements today shall save many a wrinkle and grey(s)! Would you not swap the financial and behavioral uncertainties for assured trouble-free rapport? Now sit back, as behind us lies complex conversations; What artistry goes into writing this 'Not-A-Fiction'! So, tangle the loose ends: service bills, pet policies, occupancy rules, damages, emergencies, payment protocols. Everything concerning your tenant and you, needs a mention. Declutter details into easy sections; Remember attorney while friend, just like an onion-hide-or-seek!

Your Road-Runner Rental Policies

Complementing the lease layout with your rental policies could your masterstroke. It — no kidding — is like adding an express 'Google Maps' to your rental venture! Navigation gets way easier when rules are spelled out clear and loud.

Go by the book! Identify. Remediate. Reflate. — the easy, effortless steps to create an atmosphere where your tenant can visualize a happy household, and the landlord (ding-ding, that's you!) can effortlessly manage his property. Rules sound strict? Say guidelines, swift, fluid, bound by respect and rationale.

Securing our vested assets is high on the charts of survival workouts. Picture yourself. You hold a priceless hand-knit oriental rug adorning the Buckingham vase overlooking Polish teak furniture.

Minimize fear of discretion. Look for defined curb appeal protocols which shall extend to the backyard directives limiting loud parties or excessive vehicle parking. Rental hieroglyphics could bid a joyful life for the collectibles at your property while keeping the occupant within relative freedom.

Themes of tenant safety — water and fire safety, accident prevention, ban over illicit stuff, maintaining cleanliness pair best buddies with protocols around pets and observance of silence rules specifically into the odd hours. Ultimately, adopting easy yet stern lines of policies helped serve balance the oscillating nexus of peace amongst renters and landlords.

Handling Maintenance and Repairs

It sounds pretty hefty and complicated, but trust me—it's easier than following those alien-like installation instructions from IKEA.

First things first, you definitely need a well-oiled strategy, or you'll find that unruly faucet adding up to your headaches.

Proactive Strategy

Here's first-prize thinking. Prevention is easier than reaction. Merely waiting to react when things break down will steer you quicker towards sinking your vessel rather than steering clear of icebergs (metaphorically speaking.) Try to engage in proactive property maintenance regularly. A slim expense right off the bat is better than a rupturing miscellaneous account. Makes sense, right? Plus, on top of dodging bigger costs down the line, it also keeps your tenants happier—and living in a dreary house can mimic a rain cloud hovering above everywhere they go.

Regular Inspection

Now bro, keep in mind you must establish a routine inspection, and it should be every property manager bff's diary notes. Writing this down? Good! Set dates to check all major systems and areas of the property (cue 007 music), such as heaters, ACs, roofs. Yup, even if you've got a ruthless fear of heights, you got to sell your fear stocks and buy some courage—for basics like checking shingles over bright and sunny days, and even talking about doom day-like situations like if a severe storm hits town, your wallet wouldn't shed pounds.

Inform the Tenants

Dust off that communication box and tell your tenants, potential or current, about this routine inspection plan. Open communications maintain a cordial relationship not keeping them on the edge in the middle of binge-watching Netflix just when they receive an unexpected knock on the door. Be organized, and tell them the routine checkup timings by keeping them update about all the nitty-gritty stuff. Were you thinking all of Property Management & maintenance is going to be like starring in an episode of the office with mundane protocols only? Nope, plan to reach out to tenants for any sort of repair trouble headed your way.

Prioritize Safety

Hey Sherlock, bring in your great mindful machinery amid the mystery of anticipating any damage causing a safety threat or severe property loss— face to face with such situations you need a brilliant work like Moriarty's nemesis or probably just an emergency plan. Prioritize safety checks for natural gas, heating systems and electricity, and act faster than the agents against aliens to eliminate dangers. Well, the bottom line: safety always sits on the front of maintenance and regular checklists.

Tracking System

Yeah, yeah, stuffing all those bits-and-bobs businesses in a spreadsheet gives better understanding as retrospectives ring clearer? Glad you thought so.

So, Mr. Shrewd Planner, you got to keep tabs on costs you spend on your properties— all of them for things like past repairs, inspections (remember, we just talked about it.). Plus due updates and stuff. Procure contacts of contractors, landscapers, plumbers, the gang who spins seamless technology mysticism-electricians, handymen all in one place. Now, let's name it—the ogre colored binder seems legendary now?

Dealing with Tenant Issues and Evictions

Hey pal, you remember how we used to joke about buying those extravagant beach houses when we hit the winning lottery numbers — managing palatial estates filled with potential tenants, a lot of hard work but good money? It may have started out as a joke but let's consider it on the highly likely (or nearly impossible, depending on how you interpret the joke) chance that it happens.

How much of that have you seriously thought about? Here's some of what I've found out, mostly focusing on one major "joy" of property ownership—the problematic part: difficult tenants and evictions.

Tenants and Troubles

So, we all have people trouble every now and then, no exception in property management and maintenance as well. Once you become a landlord, you'll meet a massive variety of characters. A few tenant scenarios are pretty common.

Scenario one is the Late-Ish Payers. Davey remembers Ed and Norma—tenants of his downtown place—and how they'd miss a payment deadline or two, slipping in their checks a day or two later after multiple gentle reminders.

Here's Scenario Two: more bothersome—the "Ball of Complaints". These folks honestly seem to find joy in riposting perceived injustices for everything ranging from slightly cold water to malfunctioning power sockets.

Finally, the most challenging breed of tenant is The Destroyers. Picture a pissed-off guitarist decimating his guitar after an energetic performance. Now imagine your lavish property facing the same devastating fate.

Time for Some Solutions

"Baby, do you understand me now… Sometimes ya see that I'm mad?" - This line from Nina Simone's perennial song "Don't Let Me Be Misunderstood" sums up tenants perfectly. They want to be understood, need someone who will listen to them and above all get their problems solved.

Regularly inspect your property for any potential hazards that can pose a problem. Invest in immediate maintenance activities, thus preventing these issues from occurring in the first place.

As per Davey's advice for dealing with the Late-Ish Payers, there needs to be an enforced deadline—a clause, credit or charge related to timely payments should be included in your agreement (punctual individuals even get rewarded).

A hybrid of patience and skill goes for those Ball of Complaints as well. Most importantly, address grievances adroitly. Listening attentively to their issues reduces the friction between you and the tenant while making them feel they are cared for.

Genesis' apt phrase, 'Land of Confusion,' fits The Destroyers situation, as you have to think critically in this case. Deduct from the tenant's security deposit to pay for incurred damages as instructed in the original lease agreement, and discuss with them the impacts of their actions.

Eviction Happens – Eventually

Unfortunately, despite attempts at mitigation, evictions are sometimes unavoidable—it's the harshest, reality of property management and maintenance.

Follow the Law: Jurisdiction rules abound in every territory, affecting eviction causes—late rent, excessive property damage, or maybe even illegal activities on premises. Stick to these laws. Check-lists do wonders during such situations too. Have an eviction notice at ready that clearly contains grounds for eviction, specifying the gratification needed as well expectations from the tenant's part within the notice period.

Talking Things Out: Don't short-cut to showing the boot. Try speaking with your tenant to see if you can mutually satisfy or reach an agreement. Have an open discussion rather simply delivering a legal notice. This might save costs and stress.

Proper Documentation: If eviction becomes a must, ensure you properly process all legal documentation. That guarantees protection under law and less hassle.

Chapter 8: Maximizing Rental Income
Setting Competitive Rental Rates

Just figured I'd drop some knowledge that might be handy; especially if you're contemplating being a landlord or already renting out your property but not quite getting that volume of our friend: the cash. I'm simply talking about squeezing all the potential bucks from this kind of business: Maximizing Rental Income. You know what? The jackpot question for many landlords is: How do I set my rental rates at just the right spot where they're competitive yet profitable?

But you know, just like any old friend advice, the "secret" to maximizing your property's earning capacity as a rental unit is one hell of a blend—kind of like a bloody balance of offering a lucrative deal yet all the while favored by the Queen of Wallets. Well buddy, setting competitive rental rates is a bit of an art, but more than anything, it is infused with practical mathematics and market analysis. You got to pole up and let's weigh in a bit deeper, pal.

First Thing's First— Do Your Market Research

Picture it like going fishing—you can't just head out with your rod, forgetting the bait or wrong worm for the hard-to-get salmons—who cares, throw in champagne for the posh ones, let's get 'em. Similarly, you can't just wake up and set some arbitrary prices and expect tenants to line up to pay. Crack open your trusty laptop and, nah, not for that TV series; conduct a comparative tour in the parlance of price listings. Websites like Zillow, Craigslist and real estate agents can serve your platter. Two key factors you want at shore: what the monthly rental rates are, and how quickly units are being rented out in the neighborhood. It'll give you a quick gut check on competitively populated pricing range for your type of rental unit. Say, if most units like yours are going for around $2000/month and getting rented quickly, then well, setting your little gem for $3000/month may work again—or just leave you stiff hoping each lonely month after the next.

In English: Higher rate equals longer vacancy typically.
Be Realistic

Alright, whether you like it or not, maybe your property's not a big, glitzy beacon of modern condo craftsmanship. And you know what: "That's okay!" As any friendly counselor would recommend therapist-ish way, understanding these can help us be realistic buddies. Yes, you heard me: stubborn pride goes home; deep breath and ego out. By that, what I elbow-nudge-wink suggest is: Listen to your unit's limitations and offerings & look the market right in the eye. A one-bedroom apartment in a condo building goes for, say, $1,200 per month, a similar basement suite might peak on $900/month. Asking for anything more might render an empty echo in your unit's hall sooner than hosting a gleefully paying tenant.

Add Contractual Sweetness to that Rate

Alright, first up—always protect your investment. Still golden honey word for any extra-value contractual clause: tenants-landlord monthly communication loop, right struct arrangement for any repair costs or any peeling 'ends-meet' decisions. For instance, say, you should surely be okay as a landlord if any mild and cheap repairs are paid and carried by tenants, right?

So here's where the P in 'Peace of Mind Rental Contract for Property Owners' comes to near-euphoric idea.

Take a moment and think over anything exciting to add that distinguishably sweetens your property's oomph factor. Companion titles? Monopoly (god, go literal) or Rummikub: Safe unless it's Snakes & Ladders unless really, these rare bunch exist. Whether you permit pets, offer free Wi-Fi or pile a suite full with mahogany furniture (lighten on second thought), everyone reminisces of truly personalised contracts, and these nifty additions may make offering slightly higher-than-average rental rates.

Think win-win and pile smiles both ends—tenant and your worldly-rich pockets.

Strategies for Attracting and Retaining Quality Tenants

It looks like you're interested in maximizing your rental income, right? Awesome! I've got some stellar strategies for you about attracting and keeping tip-top quality tenants. It might seem tricky at first, but trust me, with a bit of commitment, a small dash of patience, and the right approach, your property can turn into a reliable revenue stream.

Strategy #1: Prepare Your Property

First and foremost, your property is key. It should scream 'home' —— comfortable, clean, quiet, safe. Imagine if you saw that movie mousetrap maze kind of place; would you want to stay?

Definitely not, huh? So, it would be wise to ensure that all decorative and structural details are in balance and smack-dab in the middle of prime condition. Quick fixes such as painting the walls, hemming in loose edges, adorning with quality window covers, and dot-your-eyes' clean doors and floors could spell a world of difference.

Strategy #2: Price Smartly

Too high or too low, none go! Hey, that means you'll make less from your property if you overprice it because it's vacant most of the time. Chances are potential tenants will almost always find some more cost-effective alternative, and your mansion turns into that grand haunted house in the desolate hill, without the Halloween buzz. On the downside, if you underprice your property, you might fill it quickly, but you are still missing your full earning potential. It won't feel good trading $1,000 per month only to later realize you could play in the $1,200 moola-thé field. Therefore, always benchmark and price smartly.

Strategy #3: Spotlight it with Marketing

You can't whisper "thar's gold in here" and expect a crowd beating down your door with piled up leases and deposits. Nope, doesn't work that way. Get loud and proud with your listing— market it like you're trading your old vintage comics collection on eBay. Let your marketing scream 'la crème de la crème.' Esthetically engaging (G-rated of course!) photographs, detailed yet pithy property description nested in professional, short-verbatim language. Heck maybe that 'optimized SEO language with socially integrated platforms' mantra might get you some double-click tenants eager to rent ASAP! Enhance online presence with a posting on credible property listing sites. Prefer online you say? Whichever way suits your boat, fly your banner high and be sure to update should anything about the place changes (new view, better doors, garden, pavement).

Strategy #4: Credit Checks and References

There are few things more disappointing than a delinquent tenant who damages your property or who constantly defaults on rent payments. OUCH! That'll hurt the wallet. That's why it's essential imperative (take note, I gestured my pointer like Sanders preaching the Vermont Constitution here!) to do thorough background checks and ask for references. It might seem tedious at the onset, but it'll save you a load of heartache in the long run. Granted, running credit checks and asking for references can't cut out all potential problems, but you can sidestep chronic issues like consistent late rent payments, or deplorable living habits affecting tenancy longevity.

Strategy #5: Be a Responsible Landlord

Long gone are characters of Scrooge-like landlords overtaxing and under-delivering. As property-return-increasers (let's coin that for landlords!), developing solid relationships with tenants equates beneficial jackpot. Adopt a considerate, communicative, and responsive pose towards your tenants. If they message you that the bathroom sink is botched or heating is acting moody, your swift effective response if possible, reinforces trust. They'll not just stick around but even refer others. Now that doesn't mean morphing into their go-to-HVAC-guy for each task, but big hiccups require timely management.

Take care touching up properties between tenancies. A happy ex-tenant's positive reviews can influence viable potential lead magnets. Trust builds trust.

Implementing Rent Increases and Lease Renewals

You remember when we talked about your rental income? Many landlords, like you, are constantly exploring methods to maximize their income while dealing with the normal hassle and uncertainties associated with rental property ownership - damage repairs, vacating tenants, costly finance, to name a few. But guess what? The art of harnessing maximum rental income is not an enigma. It boils down to a strategic mix of rental bumps and smart lease renewals. Let's sail ahead into more insights!

Why Increase Rent?

Maximizing rental income essentially means you need to ride the wave of rent increases while being fair to your tenants. 'Fair' being the operative keyword because typically, increasing the rent provides an easy way to incrementally inflate your income without significantly infringing upon tenant occupancy. However, timing and amount are really what matter here and could be quite hard to gauge. Okay, onto some figures. Posit some cases like the underlying property area developing significantly leading to increased local property prices or an outbreak like COVID-19 bringing situation in a slump. It's often seen that landlords stumble on deciding whether to increase rent annually or biannually, pegged into reasonable limits. It all really depends on the marketplace and what your existing tenants can pay. For instance, a more stable market would translate into a lesser risk and hence more frequent jump in rents.

A common method is increasing rents annually by some rate

which is equivalent or slightly above the current consumer price index increase, typically around 2%-3%. Overall, working through negotiation with the tenant can also provide you with an idea about how much incremental costs your tenants can absorb during the lease durations.

Strategically Planning Rent Increases

Now comes the strategy part – obtaining the best outcomes involves patience, fairness and careful planning. Being progressive and frequent with rent increases – it requires balancing - it keeps you sync with the marketplace and simultaneously helps retain your tenants. Also worth noting — sudden hikes bring sudden entry of movers and can engage you in cycles of often-ceaseless periods of vacancies. This might, consequently, let you experience drastic cycles involving rushes; of preparing properties for new tenants under pressured time slabs in between departures and arrivals – which does not sound a pleasing picture.

Lease Renewals - A Core Tactic

Ever thought about the inevitable costs of acquiring 'new' over 'existing' visitors for your eCommerce site? The philosophy translates in here too. It usually costs lesser, both in terms of money and time to renew an existing lease than to find, qualify and place a wholly new tenant. Remember terminating a lease can cost you lots – spinning the brain behind cleanup costs, marketing costs, not to mention probable empty periods. You know what's best about mitigating these scenarios? Tenant retention focused tactics empowers you to facilitate affable relationships with your tenants - recurrent lease renewals often prevent painful vacancies alongside helping to gently raise the rents. It can break you free from property viewings, prospective tenant communications, background verification - go log! More importantly, it might also gift you appreciations from tenants for congenial handling.

Utilizing Technology for Efficient Property Management

If you've been feeling that your rental business hasn't been performing up to your expectations, or if you simply wish to elevate your property game a notch higher, then you've landed in the right place! I will share some neat tricks under my sleeve about leveraging technology to make your property management way more efficient. Look, we're not living in the bedrock times anymore, so let's maximize the high-speed, tech-crazed world right at our fingertips! Trust me; after comprehending the things discussed here, you'll awe yourself with the wish-you-knew-sooner experiences.

So, why is efficient property management essential?
Excellent property management isn't just about depositing checks from your rent. It's way more dynamic than that! Having busy-bees for tenants require you to be speedy and organized in addressing all sorts of issues - electrical, bills dispute, misbehaving appliances(do the laundry!), neighbour quarrels, data records, property ads - OH boy, you see where I'm going: All you would wish is to multiply yourself! Hence, efficient property management not only lightens your workload but keeps your tenants happy - both of these will ultimately juice up your rental income!

Enter: Swoosh of technology in property management!
What if you could solve all these puzzles in a single fan-mode, like opening WhatsApp or reading this grand piece of advice (yes, this!)? You guessed it, folks! In this technology-fueled era, a myriad of software and app developers have got us property managers dancing to very soulful tunes these days!

Old-but-Gold-Newly-Mould: Accounting software
Accounting: bless my souffle recipe – don't they all give us headaches? Well, not anymore! Accounting software has been a boon to businesses of all sizes - yep, and our sweet little rental territory too! From tracking tenants' payments, overdue balances, expenses – all sorted with the breeze of finely-anointed taxation calculations and financial health analyses! For starters-to-all-tech, popular software like [Quickbooks](https://quickbooks.intuit.com/) or Freshbooks can come handy. For more zealous entrepreneurs, property-specific ones like [AppFolio](https://www.appfolio.com/) await!

Run your rental rodeo: Property Management Software (PMS)
Apart from accounting, we have another kind of software – one that only manages but RULES over your property management realm. Programmed to track rent collections, resolve tenant issues, schedule property maintenance, it tries to shield you from every imaginably nagging issue that pops from your rental castle walls. Platforms like [Buildium](https://www.buildium.com/) and [Rent Manager](https://www.rentmanager.com/) have been a rage, embedding comprehensive features including lease document management and property-ad promotions!

Getting-Jiggy Remote Any-Time Judicious Monitoring

Home-Automation/Security devices have cracked technology like a glow-stick - making the process of property management more appealing to a techie-loving niche. Wireless key entries (eradicate the trouble of coordinating with elusive locksmiths), thermostats that 'govern' the usage of ACs/heaters (helps residents save quite a penny) and top of all, security cameras which offer remote-property-status checks (keep watch even while sunbathing in Bora Bora). How astounding Sound does that spectrum?

Decoding 'Decibel Hell': Noise Monitors

A rowdy party, quarrelling couple or rebellious teenagers, can bring your property's value and neighbor relationship nose-diving earthquake-like. Meet Noise Monitor : landlords' new bedtime song singer - these intelligent devices notify any sound going up the "major-disturbance" level. Silent and confidential - you are not eavesdropping on everyday life but also keeping chilling melodies in-check.

All-Knowing Rent Analysis tools

Deciding pricing for rent can get pleasantly scientific now with access to rent analysis tools dating hand-in-hand with tech bubbles feature popping out fortnightly. By sparking comparative mapping for rent among similar properties near the radius, the burden of dynamics of demand-supply formula gets shifted from you to such rainmakers. So friend, as we part ways today, but not forever, my advice is to swoop worthy innovation without dampening great caution. Decision of injecting bits and bytes still needs critical reviews, understanding of T&C's, and keen perusal of offerings enwrapped. Do mull rightly over budgets, number of properties to direct to and due diligence essentials. After all, Rome wasn't built in a day, nor will your rental empire be. However, indulge time into comprehending the power of this digital discovery well, and by George, make strides you never dreamt of making. It's rocket science – but you're more than capable of creating beautiful constellations. All the new-age tech optimism from me to you, may the sublet profits commensurate your game!

I'm so glad we've this opportunity to talk a bit about one of your main concerns, your rental income. We've all had those rough patches when it hurt to see the check shrink. And let's admit, often, we are looking for unique ways to boost our income. Well, good news! We're going to navigate through that together - brainstorming options to effectively maximize your rental income. And no, I'm not summoning you to invest in extravagant amenities or undertake drastic property improvements. Our focus will be quite the contrary, rather subtle additions like laundry facilities or storage units, that'll add value to your property and spur additional cash flow. Ready, my friend?

Turn Available Space into rentable Storage Units

First things out the gate let's discuss storage units. Hear me out. Storage, whether for bikes, furniture, seasonal items or just plain old clutter, appears trivial but you'd be surprised just how seriously tenants care. Everyone prefers an extra game of Tetris balancing spaces! Sure, your apartments are bound to lack sprawling garage or foundation chambers as often seen in stand-alone houses. But have you pondered over its ancillary spaces? What about flipping the redundant area beneath the staircase into a lockable storage? Possibly the unused basement, insulated attic space, or even the alley alongside the building? More than paint and decor, it's clever use of space that nails a lasting tenant impression. You may customize these smart storage services according to tenant requirements, property layout, thereby strategically positioning them as fascinating USPs.

Viable cheap solution focused on storage could jump your rental income by sweet percentage points without dipping a toe into the apartment's livable space. Try it, sometimes small changes are all it takes!

Laundry Facilities for those who Hate Laundry Runs

Ever fled the horror called 'laundry day' during winters? Laugh all you want but that persistent parade of clothes striding down to the local laundromat has small comforts. Imagine their ignominy running into someone they know plus being charged over odds for popping buttons! Their plight expands your scope. Enter laundry facilities right inside your property.

Equipment leasing companies can help you install coin-operated machines without heaving on capital expenditure. The resident pays for the load thereby minimizing your extra utility bills. A couple of exclusive new laundering units stashed indoors or, say a hallway washroom, ensure targeted use bearing minimal impact on residential hygiene. Keep them safe, hygienic and away from clutter, and voilà, you align functioning magnificently at peak capacity nullifying machine downtime with renter contentment. The gold? When your rental space irons out daily friction points from tenant behaviours, it attracts long-term commitments, perhaps even loyal tenants giving your property the heads up! Even within saturated rental areas, such embedded services brighten profit prospects.

Charging for Parking Spaces & Charging Stations

Residential buildings nestled in dense city neighborhoods vaguely struggle with something as obvious as inadequate parking. If off-street parking is one, covered parking niche come the winter months gradually morph from convenience to necessity! Resorting to paid parking arrangements might feel unprecedented but when open spots are like striking gold, having dedicated bays could trigger substantial splashes to your will right off the hook! Who knows like-minded eco-conscious folks could be propping their electric cars while conveniently picking upon scattered and pricey power spots? Decent rental properties perceive future wave, naturally. Extend outlets for electric car charging. Believe me, the recent bursts in EV popularity call you to rake in benefits of evolved demand. For mobile world run around plug-in autos, attributing premiums onto these charging amenities turn basics into bucks faster. Circumvent high electricity demands splitting over minimalistic monthly subscription measures. Minimal extra to tenants itself rams rental rate upwards by good margins. Overall, pulling payment for such accessible amenities implicitly displace indirect maintenance costs on utility vegetation, regular upkeeps offset with an improved revenue stream.

Chapter 9: Tax Planning and Legal Considerations

Understanding tax implications and deductions

So, today, I wanted to sit down and have a little chat about something pretty important yet puzzling - Taxes and its rainbow variety of legal considerations. By the end, I promise you'll have a straightforward, no-nonsense understanding of tax implications and deductions.

So what's the big deal with Tax Planning?

In simple terms, tax planning is all about making the best financial decisions with the aim to minimize your tax liability. That's right.

An effective tax plan ensures you won't cough up more tax money than you have to. In most cases, these result in significant monetary benefits. It sounds appealing, huh?

For instance, one minute you are getting guillotined with tax liabilities, and the next, thoughtful tax planning parachutes you straight into a financial cushion. But, hang on a second - It's not just about saving a fast buck. A solid tax plan should optimize your finances over a longer period, too. Pretty amazing, isn't it?

Anyhow, if tax planning was a cake, then the sheer variety of legal considerations would be the sweet and subtly chaotic icing mixed with sprinkles.

Tax Legal Considerations

When we play the game of taxes, knowing the rules (yep, by these, we mean legal considerations) is paramount. This not only includes national laws but also your state-specific ones — Yes, as tedious as it sounds.

Let's stick with retirement plans, for example. Certain tax laws allow you to pour cash into traditional IRA's and 401(k)'s tax-free. Only when you withdraw does Uncle Sam get handsy with your treasure chest!

Look, not one to sound preachy, but overlooking legal considerations can produce very unwelcome results. Between penalties, a frantic last-minute scramble during tax season, and our pal mister audit - the consequences can be quite dire.

Now with rules in our pocket, let's get on to the most fun part,

TAX DEDUCTIONS!
Tour into the world of deductions

Bird's eye-view - Deductions equal less Tax. Picture it like a grand sale on your tax liability. More deductions you can score, greater your savings.

But, how on Earth do we land these tax-saving opportunities? Listen up! Here's a secret. Your 'ordinary' life is full of these beautiful gems. Let's mine up!

Earn some interest for yourself from those Banking guys? Ka-Ching!

Work from home maestro like I am? Your home office and associated utility bills could be a gold mine of deductions!

Got yourself Medical Insurance or spent on medical expenses? Your consideration for your health might just earn you deductions.

Cheesy line alert, but, In the world of taxes, every penny counts, actually, every deductible penny counts. Any whiff of deductions, run like a hound with it! Consider it a Taxpayers' Golden Rule.

Before the pen drops, remember, all deductions are only permissible as per the IRS rules. As Uncle Ben rightly put; With great deductions, come great substantiations. Lawfully record and audit your financials to escape any IRS kind of trouble.

Don't fret from a rare note payable or additional tax; Tax Planning isn't a wand casting magic out of blue. It's there to straighten the crippled tax structures within your financial well-being. Profitable, legal, ethical - that's Tax Planning.

Forming the right legal entity for property ownership

I was thinking we should have a little chat today about tax planning and something a little bit legalistic, but incredibly useful to understand - how we go about structuring the proper legal entity for owning a property. Trust me; it's more exciting than it might sound at first as it might end up in better fiscal health.

Be sure to do your research

First, let's be clear, it's essential that you dig deeper when it comes to legal and financial matters like this. While I'm sharing some general thoughts, do get legal or financial advice before making decisions. Now with that disclosure out the way, let's get into it.

Duration may not always matter

Normally, when you're buying a property duration might matter (that 30-year fixed mortgage, anyone?), but this is an area where it doesn't make much a whole lot of difference, whether for a short-term or long-term. The principle remains pretty much the same - Structuring your ownership allows you to plan for taxes and protect your personal and financial interests.

Corporations are not your only choice

You may first think about setting up a corporation. Corporations can be tricky, however, and can lead to an unexpected thing called 'double taxation'. That's where both the company profits and your income or dividends get taxed. Not ideal, right?

A look at legal entities

Suppose you're planning to buy a property, either for personal use, investment, or to run a business. In that case, your choices for legal entities include Sole Proprietorship, Partnership (which can be General or Limited), Corporation (C or S), and Limited Liability Company (LLC). Yeah, a real alphabet soup.

In simplest terms:

Sole Proprietorship is you alone owning everything, which comes with unlimited liability ('gulp!') if things don't go well.

Partnership spreads the responsibility but still can open partners to that unnerving 'unlimited liability' if you happen to go with General Partnership. With a Limited Partnership, on the other hand, you limit liability equivalent to what you invest.

Corporations offer a buffer where you, as an owner, aren't liable personally. The downside with Corporations though, is that ever unpopular 'double taxation' for C Corporations which most of us try to avoid. S Corporations is you, behaving like a corporation, but Uncle Sam counts you as a unique entity and wins the day just doing single-tax ('huzzah!').

A Limited Liability Company (LLC) combines facets of corporations and partnership - shelters you personally from financial obligations AND appeals to the 'tax-man' with benefits of 'pass-through' taxation ('hurrah!').

Everyone love candies but do benefits taste better?

Considering all this, many property owners have found, ideally, LLC seems to be the most tax-efficient and risk-limited route. It offers the benefit of pass-through taxation, just like a sole proprietorship or a partnership. However, it also provides the liability protection akin to a corporation. Owners only pay income taxes on earnings leaving the company in the form of salaries, dividends, etc., and the LLC itself doesn't face any corporation tax rates.

Additional benefits include dividing benefits of a business

proportionally or disproportionately among the owners due to unequal input. LLCs aren't held bound by the rigid record fundamentals enforced on corporations but should maintain fundamental records, which brings lesser threat and hassles.

Take care of your house(state) too

However, besides the type of business entity, we also need to consider state laws where the property resides. Formalizing an entity fundamentally means that you are taking part in a state's legal structure. Whether you're present on-premises or running it from afar, you become part of that state's economic system anyways. You need to ensure that your legal structure doesn't collide with the policies established(the porch doesn't smash into the house).

Ring Uncle Sam's Doorbell before his call comes

Make sure to understand the responsibilities of associations mapped according to your legal entity. Might sound basic, but believe me, many people forget and mess up, and this one thing can pop-open a trouble can that nobody wants. Briefing of roles, filing business, keeping documents aboard, embracing equitable compensation, interconnecting benefits structure, and deploying an easy procedure system equips others to gaze into structure-status.

Complying with local rental regulations and laws

You reap the twin benefits of constant income flow and capital appreciation (the increase in property value), sounds like a real money-spinner, right?

But— and here's a low tone "but", there's more to it than meets the eye. Evidently visible are tax considerations and consequential legal stipulations hidden behind the curtains. Boring, I admit! However, can't skate round these—or what's generally known, as life tends to leap out with surprises.

(Uncomfortably exhale), ok relax buddy... If I can wade through this, you certainly can too. So arm up with my arm-chair guide to tax planning and legal aspects of your real estate invasion, and let's figure this out together.

Tax planning

In tax land, long-term plays deliver fat pay short term desires fail with high tax waivers. Put in plain language, tax planning is playing smartly to limit your tax liability by benefitting from the allowances, dips, grants, exclusions and concessions ingrained in tax laws. This is perfectly legitimate; doesn't embody transgression, as is typically painted.

Now, don't get me wrong—I am not suggesting you should evade tax, that'd amount to blasting-off fraud alarm, attracting legal repercussions. Let's stay in safe harbor; yes, tax planning doesn't shake hands with avoiding due tax bills nor slipping away from reporting transactions.

Puzzling Property Taxes — Solved

Rental income rings 'ka-ching'…yet wait—you can't stash the entire cash into your pocket because Uncle Sam's expecting his share.

Tenant rents are treated as income. Earning $600 or more per year harvests a 1099-MISC form —your tax-id flagged to IRS. Filing deadline typically bites April's heel so please don't play the rabbit, take the turtle's place to redeem the form. Relish deductions, allowable expenses chiseled - interests (mortgages & loans), repairs, insurance premiums, professional dues, advertising costs, paid utilities, 'n' more to juggle down your monetary chunk to oblivious minimum. Oh, and depreciation's a magical wand directly tied to your profit abacus. It's a metaphor y'know—the property doesn't physically cry-down but IRS permutes you into casting the spell - slightly advanced topic, we'll visit later.

Your cutting-edge transactions classifying 'Passive Income' or 'Trade Business' live by different tax forms. Airbnb, VRBO slips to Schedule-E, the local rental to Schedule-C. Property 'rent-out' single days or multiple patches owe prescribed percentage in hotel taxes or transient occupancy tax, considering the city laws. Property sales tax tend to curl into spider-webs, treacherous on edges, severe to blur real profits. Short lived possessions weave into net investment income capped in net gains exacting 3.8% over $200,000 (for individuals) - smart reasoning to buckle-in under exceptions? Flip schemes excelling 12 months go under long-term capital gains astutely charged at supervised graduations. The trio spoils ain't play pretty; a) Defer tax via to 1031 tax-exchange slipping over property purchases, obliging obvious specific rules, or b) Trade life situations counting like-kind for residential, tax free indulgence. The keen behind 'Like-Type' residencies rip benefits for residence over two of five years entitled home sales to exclude $500,000 (shared) off the capital gains hook. Relief or hardship events throw light at additional deductions— consultancy advised. Tax professionals consult setting legal entities advocating privacy benefits looped with potential tax benefits if situations glove the requirements.

Abide by rental regulations

Toss the casino dice, don't pick cherries too soon, rein in the exposure of infractions prompt to destabilize your new property and tarnish prospects. Harmony sings compliance to guidelines inscribed in 'Local Zoning laws', humming tune for wanted "rental licenses," requires accurate building permits and rightfully follow state-imposed health-safety dictations. Uphold tenant dignity/freedoms binding Federal, state Fair Housing provisions; kick stereotypes— no flavor for discrimination inked under color, race, familial status, national origins, religion or disability confirming residence rentals.

Some cities post draconic laws decoding caps tied to short-term rentals or approval strict laws. Journey thru' eviction & rental collection, hammer down deposits guiding rent record /receipt/security obligations or lodger's denied service notices over contract termination, further asserting in defined rental set provisions meticulously drafted.

Legal Wrangles and I dotting

Ensure two-leveled structural/fire insurance fitting the optimum necessitates— cost/market-value. Discourse extended policies, they shield sliver-catches over fence-protrusion disputes, personal-injury/property-damage drawn via unavoidable circumstances driving unhappy dwelling.

Welcomed inspector docks add health-sales clips supplementing post-inspections assisting diminished future-proof pest/regulatory hits. Rental stipulations count first, empower comprehensive lease agreements typically drafted via attested operations defining custom attributes posted over paired observances — daily operations, property forte or State enactments.

Insurance coverage and liability protection

So, you know how usually we do our movie nights or geek out over the latest Star Wars movie release? Today is different. Let's swap Sith Lords for detailed talks on 'tax planning' and 'insurance.' Dull? Perhaps. Critical? One hundred percent, yes!

Tax Planning; Yes, It's Necessary!

I bet you've smirked at the 43rd screen of a Skyrim game and planned your next Magic: The Gathering rule-breaking move. Feels good, right? That simple act of having control over the circumstances. What if I told you that life too can become incredibly strategic once you 'get it.' And one high place to acquire control is tax planning.

Tax planning is nothing too spooky. This is big talk for controlling your financial state. It means strategically brainstorming and taking necessary fiscal choices to reduce the tax liability, so Uncle Sam gets fewer dollars. Sure, there are gory details when tax codes loom larger than your big brother's infectious smiles, but who joins a party to talk about tax regulations?

Despite its Popularity, Insurance isn't MTV…Regardless…it's in High Demand

Remember Disneyland? You compared Magic Mountain to hypothermia if you died on that voyage. Funny enough, in your case that hypothermia provides shielding. Life is all an unpredictable journey—we live it on happenstance—highs and lows coming our way. One quality investment you make for those unpredictable waves is insurance.

Getting health, life, property or auto insurance coverage, creates your financial safety pool. It's like driving "Cars" animated by Pixar as Lightning McQueen wearing a six-layered protective aura. Here's what's actually groovy about insurance. The expense you make acquiring it: the insurance premium payments, are regularly tax-deductible. That means more leverage in tax planning. How's that for screwing a fiscal light bulb?

Overcoming the Daunting Tangle of Legal Jargon

The devil lies in details. Don't be charged off by the heavy-sounding legal lingo. The law isn't only about quoting heavy Latin phrases or spouting Lex Luthor phrases—it revolves around the idea of protection.

The "*Legal Liability Protection*" in insurance sounds like heavy armor for metallic robots in an unknown, jeopardous Cybertron world. Yet its goal is to play The Guardian to your fiscal galaxy. It covers the safe from expensive misfortunes—bam! One less thing to worry about while trying to focus on getting your dividends.

A coverage limit is a part that feels tricky. It indeed sounds like an eco-friendly asteroid hitting your ship. It supports the liability (the amount you owe) should anyone claim insurance from you—something like telling a cruel G.I. Joe enemy, "You've gone far enough. No further!"

Often your coverage limit amounts and liability obligations make way on your pre-set budget eggshells. Should that limit you face become unbearable, there's an additional fortress available for convenience—yes, your Virtual Wonderworld grows! Herein 'Umbrella Policies' come into action. When your Star Cruiser gets beyond insurance's standard policy limit, umbrella policies, or extra liability, step into the play.

In simple jester-alien language, it signifies merging layers of coverage 'Till All Is ONE!' Better imagine your transformer shifting to a more colossal mode when the streets get brutal. All of these policies hold weight when stashing your taxable income; hence help in effective tax planning.

Insurance Premiums—the Beacon Corp Financial Slide

Insurance operates pretty simply: protection of wealth during unwanted wails. Thing is, wealth comes with taxes. Premiums you pay as part of insurance become deductible. That means these aren't taxes you need to let the republic milk off your hard work. There are a few blurry lines here about the types of 'covered insurances,' so it's optimized to saddle up some professional guidance.

Leveraging Personal Expenses

Here's where talk taxes coincide with everyday Joe's vade mecum: Jargon free version of things would sound like buy health insurance, you can leach off their expenses as deductions.

Welcome to tax planning 101!

Officers spending higher sums on medical, like your hypochondriac mom when a coughing menace seemed an impossible enemy in a Subway Surfers background, may project for this deduction.

Increase your deductible privilege or 'self-insure' odd surprises on the health front. Kinky Roth Ira retirement services allow for distributed, tax-free medical expenses as well!
Socially Influencing Taxes — Self-Employed and Heroes with Business Stardom

Remember when bosses revolved around higher realms alone, deemed mighty on an isolated cloud? Well mingle with the realities now as being self-employed or managing a self-started venture provides bounties on Health Insurance deductions. Fluctuations buzz all over, but at a significant percentage on their Taxable Tax to the federal beings.

Small insured businesses qualify for relatively valued tax credits. The coverage proves a godsend. If you receive insurance via an employment exchange or approach Obamacare (Just like your Gandalf, bringing hope no matter what), you'd notch up percentage credits, too.

The flexibility of insurance coverage merges the unsolved maze of tax planning and legal liability essentials cleanly. So without biting more boom-bangs, wrap financial safety protocols giving you iron fists in an often dwindling game of wealth and finance!
Now that the seemingly dull conversation is over, go ahead! Unsheathe your Cards against Humanity: World Wide Web packs, and be gentle like Bitcoin while beating the mortgage bloat. You'll kill it! Just putting it beyond the Sith Lord stats makes you...grand, doesn't it? Make it real. So buckle up for a secure joyride on the shiny financial glimmer streets.

Chapter 10: Scaling Your Rental Property Portfolio

Assessing portfolio growth strategies

It All Starts with Having a Concrete Plan

Doesn't everything?

As spontaneous as a vacation to the Maldives sounds, you got to plan it for costing's sake or not run stuck midway. Likewise, a well-thought-out plan is your golden ticket in property-business growth. Lets snipe down to some of the components of this plan.

Goals: Know what you want to achieve—buy and hold riches, i.e., long term gains, or instant resale profits?

Risk Patience: Understand your temperament towards risk. What's the maximum level of risk you can bear without fretting bug-eyed every night?

Financial Skyline: Ensure a concrete view of what your financial landscape looks like. Understanding your investments, liabilities, assets, expenditures—et al.

Next recall the pertinent mantra— 'Location, Location, Location.' Am I sounding a bit clichéd? But it is the underlying truth; locality sets the tone of your investment returns. So research intensively on the exact locations like a hungry hawk, and astuteness is your key here.

Mentoring Saves Mets and Bets

Ninety-nine issues but a mentor ain't one!

Trust me when I say this, these folks are your Yoda in this big-bad-boogie of real estate ventures. Industry veterans will know the nooks and hacks and have seen bubbles risen bust in real life. So sniff out for one. Read up as many experiences till Google tires, listen to growth experiences directly from horse's mouth. A mentor can give you so much insight into what worked, and most importantly, what didn't.

Acquiring More Properties

Acquiring more rental properties is clearly your most natural next step towards growing your portfolio. But climbing this ladder isn't devoid of threats. A single wrong purchase risks not only corrosive drainage of assets but is soul-sapping.

Being educated is time consuming but worth every single dime! Falling prey to attractive 'outside offerings', obscure financing alternatives, big-no-flashing red flags like too good to be true deals should get required examination.

Also, do stick to an age-old industry technique - buy below market value to prevent running deep waters under strenuous economic circumstances.

Minimize Vacancies

This matter—and big time! Long vacancies leave ripples in your revenue flow and upset the apple cart of your mortgage repayments, which never seem to take a break, no?

Simple techniques can minimize vacancies. Improve your curb appeal because first impressions do count. Speed up tenant-responsive necessities, and running great tenant service is up your street for a good tenant retention rate.

Spice up With Cost Efficiency

An interesting route to manifold your rental property portfolio isn't always just about bigger numbers acquisition. You might be surprised how giving that extra attentiveness heeds to cost efficiency could act as a marvelous genie. Consistently updating interior fixtures, installing energy-efficient amenities, periodic maintenances might seem overheads but in reality, fall an inch short of colossal repair costs.

Didn't Mother always emphasize savings? And yeah, a stitch in time does indeed save nine.

Leveraging Management Skills

As your keys clink becoming harder to singlehandedly maintain, property managers enter the battle, their superpower being taking away all your groundwork ordeal. Check references, light-prompt management fees audits, perform meticulous scrutinizes for the best!

Steady Tenant Flow with Marketing

An underestimated masterstroke is marketing prowess—a quick pic n mix ad search on community messages across all search plateaus. Now tenant inquiries jingling your phone—happy churn nightmares to Cinderella dreams.

It takes determination, focus but most importantly, a strategy. And that strategy folks, is none other than scaling your rental property portfolio. You don't get it? No problem at all, let's get started.

UNDERSTANDING SCALING
What is Scaling?
Before your brain starts conjuring odd chain concept images, let me quickly make this clear. By scaling, I mean growing or expanding your rental property business. This growth may involve buying up as many properties as your funds allow or otherwise leveraging existing properties to buy more. .

Who can Scale?
Not to sound touristic, but everybody can scale as long they commit to understanding and playing their cards right. Dad just green-lighted a minor fortune for you? Scale! Just won the lottery? Food for thought - scale! Want a secure investment for your hard-earned money? You guessed it, buddy - scale!

FINANCING MULTIPLE PROPERTIES
Often, this is where folks face off with the big, bad wolf. Sharks in the financial ocean may leave feeling aggrieved. You're not even sure how to fund the first rental property, much less having a portfolio, eh? Well, that's what friends are for, let's take this through together.

Groundwork
Understanding Capital
An interplay between your cash-in hand and a suitable financial partnership brings about successful scaling. Mystified? Don't be! Your own dough, paired with the right kind of funding, sets up the foundation for purchasing properties. Of course, the denser your equity in existing properties, the better the position for receiving funds.

Credit Rating
Psst, buddy - a note. Trying to assemble uber-cool properties shouldn't trip down your credit score. Always monitor your credit rating - it's a ticket for attracting lenders or fiancées, LOL. Ensure a good, clean financial history with every subsequent property purchased.

The Money Part: How to Fund Your Properties
Still with me? Excellent! Now let's dig into the part we've all been waiting for - money! Here are some routes to explore:

Traditional Banks

Remember Uncle Scrooge's load of cash vault in the comic, Duck Tales? Well, imaginary or not, banks have no scarcity of funds. They are amongst the chief sources for sourcing investments. While they conduct enough audits ensuring cold sweat, a strong financial stability and a spoonful of patience might just convince these folks to root for you. Though interest rates might come attached with all this bank moolah. Be prepared!

Private Financing

Got wealthy friends whose biggest problem is where to invest? Present an attractive plan about this rollercoaster of a game. Private financing helps steer large projects smoothly without institutional busybodies. Additionally, terms are negotiable, and proceedings sail forward smoothly - given the hand of friendship extended from investor to investee ;)

Hard Money Lenders

Hey, nothing hard about grasping hard money lenders. They are professional money lenders, typically not associated with banks, focusing mainly on the potential property rather than the ambiguity of the borrower. Since they operate over short terms, remember that owning tangible property after arranging financing, becomes crucial.

Owner Financing

Not frequent, but in sectors where property shelf life exceeds traditional periods, owners might agree to financing arrangements themselves. Patience can ride victorious with seller availability, making owner financing a smooth pact.

Private Mortgage

Explicitly functions for purchasing house or flat where lender presents consent for land act registration paid by borrower. Premier for a homely entry into the world of rental properties, I'll say.

Home Equity Line of Credit (HELOC)

Akin to credit card usage on the foundation of home equity, it's a route to tap into for debt consolidation or home improvements best. Range depending on your outstanding debt, market value and existing mortgages.

Remember guys and gals, this quest becomes an epic when you begin appreciating the "big picture". Balance logic of costs, possibilities of profits as all spaces would not you expected returns. In conclusion, patience, strategy-building, and cooperation with potential fund-providers will help pull off a striking rental property portfolio.

This time round let's delve deeper, we're moving beyond the concept of not having just one rental property but several, yes you heard me right, multiple baby! Congrats buddy, you've hit the true investor status.

Think of that potential income flow (steady, and monthly! now that really must feel good!). Dreamy right? While in the same light potentially scary because…come on guys, the mere thought of managing multiple properties might seem like a headache and quite demanding. But hold up, let me share some secret sauce here. Relax, sip your coffee, and let's dive in.

Why You Need Property Managers
(Believe me, you won't Regret It)

Remember the time we were discussing that getting the perfect tenant was like finding that ultimate streaming platform that catered to all our crazy movie preferences, romantic comedies, sci-fi, actions blend them all, a perfect concoction? The same applies here, finding a great property manager is similar in all proportions. Yeah, you didn't think the metaphoric analysis could get crazier?

Allow me to blow your mind, imagine a scenario where you no longer have to hear tenants' midnight woes about a pesky faucet that would not stop ticking. Or worse than worst argument ever - apartments A and B arguing over parking spaces. Ha! Now that doesn't seem fun, doesn't it?

Here is why brilliant property managers come in:

1. Tenant Mumbo Jumbo: Seriously a property manager will fix all tenant issues in a snap. Like magic.

2. Time is Treasure: An efficient property manager will simply free up your time to strategies, plan, navigate and ultimately enjoy the fruits of your wise investments—or simply just have time off.

3. Listing Marvel: Listing your property in an attractive, best-priced marketable manner can indeed bring you the elite of tenants out there. Property managers are equipped with superior advertising tools to accomplish this objective.

Building A Team: Rocking the Dream with Human Capital Preservation

Being an investor is a hectic business calling one for constant planning, execution and formulating strategies. Scaling up your rental property portfolio is pure madness without the help of your team. It isn't any kind of team, rather you need a 'Dream' team. Let's help you channel your inner 'Money Heist Professor', shall we?

1. Choose Expert Members: Establish experts at various fields in your circle of influence. A seasoned handyman for the hard tasks, an experienced attorney for the daunting legal matters, a financial adviser or tax specialist to handle all number wizardry… so technically guys, talking about LeBron James caliber in their respective roles.

2. Foster Your Team Endurance: Mutual Interests brings in a binding loyalty, endurance ensuring a win-win situation for all and sundry. Therefore, it's crucial for the team fee structures to be designed in such an appealing and beneficial way to foster an enduring team.

3. Host Regular Team Meetings: Yes, it may sound exhausting but think of these periods as oil refueling times for your portfolio car engine. Meetings will galvanize strategic discussions, brainstorming and the ultimate crystal-clear execution of set blueprint for scaling investment intelligence—"Remember Unity Is Strength"

Undoubtedly, scaling your rental property portfolio calls for forthright plans, skilled selection strategy and yea, a lot of caffeine (or whatever floats your boat). Here's to today's learning and laughs! So grab the after-moon drinks, guys and cheers to "many properties in your portfolio and many more in your dreams".

Remember, mastering and managing domains out here as a property investor need team support for success—think of it as plain old marriage, "for better or worse but definitely worth the ride."

Remember Superman without a Lois is nude without his glasses. Billionaires never go to war without their soldiers, do they? The point is buddy, sooner or later, professionals must come aboard to ride the rough dynamics of property investment.

Evaluating the potential for diversification

The Rationale for Diversification

"Why should I concern myself with diversifying?" One may wonder. As an investor, your main threats are risk and concentrating all your resources in a single area. By expanding your rental property portfolio into various markets, property types and investment strategies, you can decrease the risk associated with your investment and potentially improve profitability.

For instance, if every property in your portfolio is identical, based in the same neighborhood, or caters to the same types of tenants - a downturn in that particular market, demographic shift, or even a legislative change affecting that unit type can decimate your returns. And my friend, we definitely do not want that. By diversifying, you can cushion that blow and keep the cash flow running, come rain or shine.

Balancing Your Inventory

As with any business, balance is key. Here's where diversification comes in. Mixing it up in terms of locale, size, price range along with short and long-term leases will give you exposure to various client categories and revenue streams. Think of it like owning a fruit stand instead of just selling apples.
Having more property types attracts a broader range of tenants and can stabilize your income. If half of your units are family-focused, but there's a slow-down in that market, you won't be feeling the heat as long as the other half of your inventory - maybe studios for young professionals - remains in high demand. You catch my drift?

Geography – Don't Be Afraid to Cast your Net Wider

On another note, I notice a lot of first-timers focusing their efforts exclusively within neighboring cities or towns. Now, doing so does have definite benefits such as knowledge of the local market, ease of self-management, and keeping maintenance costs in check. But it's a common misbelief that excellent real estate investments are solely found a stone's throw away. When residential yields begin to dried up locally, it might be worth keeping tabs on out-of-state or even overseas property markets. Do bear in mind, a wide-spread investment means you'll be spreading yourself wide too. Client meeting in the east, maintenance problems in the west? Sounds chaotic. Hence why, getting proficient property management firms onboard surely becomes inevitable for managing long-distance assets.

Commercial and Single-Family Homes: Yin and Yang of Property Investment

Continuing on the theme of diversity, have you ever thought about venturing into commercial real estate (CRE) in your portfolio? True, they can be trickier and exceptional detail-oriented. It means deciphering complicated lease agreements and getting familiar with niche markets. So, a bumpier learning curve ahead. Why trouble yourself? Well, the advantages mostly lie in the numbers. Longer lease durations lead to more consistent income, and also have the plus point of higher average returns compared with single-family homes. But here's a cool fact: some matters like on-site maintenance often become the tenant's responsibility - how handy is that?

Does this mean waving goodbye to the familiar comforts of residential property investment? Certainly not! The order of the property universe calls for balance. Single-family homes, after all, are faster to rent due to the evergreen demand, easier to manage, and a residential mortgage is simpler to secure than the commercial counterparts. Ergo, integrating commercial holdings along with your residential properties can again help you achieve equilibrium and optimize stability in returns.

Never Forget to Assess Risk

Commit this to memory — diversification ≠ total risk eradication. Rerouting investments in multiple directions introduces variety of risks. Geography-wise, a location great today may not be appealing tomorrow, or a seemingly burgeoning cafe cum bookstore sector (in case of CRE) might just spiral downwards. Translation: diversification should walk arm-in-arm with deep analysis of prospective markets & properties, or there's trouble ahead.

Chapter 11: Real Estate Market Cycles and Strategies

Recognizing market cycles and their impact on rental properties

Like all types of markets, weather be it apple sales, solar panels, cars, film releases or services; real estate values are volatile, they fluctuate. There is truly no spell-protected straight road. What intimidates is the unpredictability of these market cycles. They distinctly recycle into four stages – Recovery, Expansion, Hyper Supply, and Recession. Wouldn't it be an absolute piece of cake (city cyclist analogy incoming!) to be aware of the upcoming potholes or speed graphs before you decide to cycle downtown?

Let's look at those stages now, not like another tiresome economics seminar, but intuitively understanding what industries naturally go through.

Recovery

This stage sneaks in after a cherry bottom-low property market. At this point, the majority of people gel as a rather timid flock. Now, don't get me wrong, adverse weather isn't the time to sally forth newbie-cycling mode on, but if you keep the prospect of trailing winds, simplified road sloping, and a rather visible street to cycle healthy, recovering markets have the time advantage.

While the laggards unduly concerned with another possible downturn usually retreat, recovery timestamps can hold some pretty outstanding penny-saving, purchasing real estate opportunities. Unemployment figure tread either stable plateaus or desist tone signaling for the market to fill necessary demand. Drawing bike analyte again, if you strap on those well-informed security pads (research data, market experts or real numbers), making way ahead wouldn't feel unviable.

Expansion

This is slightly uphill cycling experience, packed cool with ideal pedaling balance. Roaring cranes on construction sites, vast spikes in occupation growth or constant tenant inquiries work are beacons for such weather parameters. As the recovery phase consummates towards lower risks and returns a toe healthier, speculative investors dive into putting money on developmental projects or scaling onto higher returns.

Territorial selection here vitalizes important landscapes to strategies upon – be it metropolitan centers, suburbs or rural pin-asides on maps. Buoyant availability or durability paths a better landscape for future scenarios: Short term leasing (high on pocket rental collects), property flipping (remodel and resale on ascending market prices), vacation rentals or college-centric buys.

Hyper Supply

When you can vision a downhill distance, certain you can paddle up acceleration needed, but there needs clocking well because the descent won't shy in pinning challenges after. There ascends a conspicuous newer supply, the occupancy treads may stagger constant, but demand rains start slowing. Construction climax may hint to no tomorrow's scale, turn wary, spot and follow the hyperextension for hyper supply check just before its midnight hue. If you're already spinning returns by this juncture, perceptive outlook would have realized maximized profits preventable. Downswing risks forge from not trailing these market indicators – cautious lodging onto counter-cyclic investing might save being knee-deep under quicksand draining possible profits.

Recession

Sometimes you invariably collide, cycle rams to tumble through and pans to harsh realities. Tenants find chasing sustenance tricky, vacancies usher thin market profiles pandering misery for your bank scores. Even the enthusiastic markets can slump to suffocate. But this can mask as also the opportunity guy, for you can invest little seeking apparent profits yet acquire foundational steps for long-sighted profits during nurturer periods.

Wrapping bites into the conversation, proper strategies revolve the rental market nuances on cyclical awareness and adopting solid pragmatism minus any risk susceptibility. There'll inevitably rain times constricted by restrictions, judicious monetizing dynamics, stressing economies or rules upscaling odds, take everything with a pinch of salt.

Sailing wiser through estate market panning out better perceptions towards resourceful ventures works ahead, rental-wise. A bird's eye maps growth employing time justice, attentive detouring and priming mites on troves like property condition or amenities. The key is carving creative solutions perceptive of incoming pitfalls or rising opportunities, a traditional real outlook accommodating insightful capital or managing marquee tenant strategies.

Keep at uncovering robust tenants despite constant stages at varying rental cycles, conventional systems aren't enemy holograms. Lock strategies on target running assets as self-measuring geodesic circles toward sustained patios of successes. Safely respond to circumstantial tufts scraping markets readdressing a boom or doom spectrum with recovery or recession ally affected weathers.

Adapting strategies for different market conditions

Surviving the Real Estate Hurricane

Let's agree on one thing — the real estate market can be as fickle and unpredictable as a dude who's decided to finally construct that model of Tower Bridge he purchased a while back. Heck, whether you're contemplating investing, buying a property, or even mapping new office rentals, various cycles can turn your awesome real-estate smile upside down.

To be as effective as possible, we need tactics that work in ALL seasons, adjusting smoothly for market heats (cue soaring sales!") and cools ("Oof, cold shoulder!"). But fret not; as real estate investors like us, it's more about making informed decisions than possessing crystal balls.

Understanding the Real Estate Market Cycles

Tailoring strategies according to real estate market cycles can feel like attempting to fit a square peg in a round hole. But once we "get it" like Adele, everything falls in its place. So here's the tea: Boom Phase: Picture a summer fair bustling with eager investors and transactions. This is the phase offering the highest property demand and quickest home sales. Trendy neighbourhoods? Skyrocketing home prices? New construction? You bet!

Slump Phase: Ladies and mates, we've hit rocky ground here- a downswing of buyer activity and dropping prices, summoning a market downturn. (It'll pass, I promise!)

Bust Phase: Definitely a tougher phase, it may involve foreclosures, fewer construction, and faint-hearted sellers. Do we lose hope? Absolutely not! Remember, we're strategy-evolved! Rebirth Phase: Inspired by the compelling urge of getting back on its feet, this phase sees revitalized opportunities and recovering sales.

Investors who master these distinct cycles and their market characteristics bear fruit.

Tailoring Strategies According to Market Conditions

Now, let's hop the tram and do a rundown of some dynamite strategies for each cycle phase.

Boom Phase- Flipping: We isn't talking flipping pancakes or skateboards (though both are cool). Flipping in real estate is purchasing a property and reselling it soon at a much higher profit thanks to rising market trends. However, remember- mind your budget!

Slump Phase- Go the Wholesale Route: Negotiate a contract to buy a property at a low cost, then pass this contract to another buyer, often rehabbers or landlords, pocketing modest profit for your matchmaking.

Bust Phase- Buy-and-Hold Rentals: With lower property prices, it might be a good idea to flash your buy-ability. Simply, buy a property in the bust phase, rent it out, and patience.exe until it hatches into a cash-generating asset.

Rebirth Phase- Invest in Development: If prices are still recovering, we can put money into developing more low-cost yet productive/innovative property developments.

Before embracing any strategy, remember, it's key to understand our own risk tolerance, investment savvy, and time commitment.

Identifying opportunities in a buyer's or seller's market

There's some great conversation that's been taking place recently about the ever-changing real estate market, and I thought you might want to join in. Let's dive into both the buyer's and seller's market overall — know when each happens and how you can take advantage.

Picking up on the Market Pulse

First thing's first, it's essential to understand the market. Trust me, getting to grips with it is simpler than it sounds. Let's pretend for a minute that the real estate market is a beach volleyball match – it's all about if the 'ball' or the opportunity, is in your court or not. An easier comparison? All right then, Picture that there's either more shells (houses up for grabs) than tourists (buyers) – a buyer's market, or vice-versa - a seller's market. In addition to deciding who's got the upper hand in the market, these terms demonstrate potential opportunities or challenges for both buyers and sellers.

Jingle all the way in Buyer's Market

Straight off the bat, a buyer's market happens when there are more homes for sale than there are people looking to buy. Prices typically go down, giving you a chance to score a good deal. Traditional cash may be scarce in this market, but an abundance of choice is certainly in - sounds like Jingle Bells in July!

Plenty of things contribute to a buyer's market; declining

neighborhoods or high-interest rates for example. But these circumstances are not always bad for interested buyers.

Ever tried haggling at a market, hoping for a discount? Imagine yourself walking along aisles filled with your favorites - shiny apples and strawberries put up in a convincing display. With many similar options, the ball, or the bargaining chip, is in your court. And the vendors (or property sellers)… they're eager to close the deal since stocks are high. Translate this to a buyer's market scenario in real estate, and you've cracked the entire process! What you're picturing in your head now can work wonders with your negotiation. It requires a keen eye to recognize properties with potential. Some may view a declining neighborhood as a burden. A visionary like you? It's a golden opportunity cleverly disguised. Someone could sell you that lemon (house) at a steal, and with a little sugar (renovation), you have yourself a tasty lemonade (an attractive changed property)!

Patience plays a key role in this market. It might need seasoning, a wait equal to slow cooking that results in a flavorful pot of opportunities. Take your time, see potentially undervalued real properties. In the end, a smart move involves one that might be counter intuitive - "buy when others are selling and sell when others are buying".

Sense the Seller's Superpowers

Flip the coin, and let's move on to a seller's market. Picture the same apples and strawberries on sale, only this time, it's swarming with clutching customers while apples are insufficient. This means high competition among buyers and possibly sparking a 'bidding war'. Even though market conditions seem to favor sellers here, home seekers can still get a piece of the pie - the game isn't over, pal. Curiosity may ask, "Why the frenzy?" Remember, an over-supply may lead to reduced prices or the buyer's market. So the reverse also applies, right? You got it – A home under-supply amps up the selling price, pushing towards a seller's market. Yet, participating in the game at all can be a strategy. Sounds nonsensical, right? Think about this; more generous loans sprout in a surcharged economy, thus higher purchase opportunities. During a seller's market where property demands peak, property prices do too. Surprising to some, a stable income during such times paired with your financial thriftiness can translate to

bargaining levers. Say "Open Sesame," buddy, and behold, opened doors to good loan opportunities!
Actively participating has another benefit. True, the real-estate crown may currently belong to the sellers. But the real craft lies in adopting a future-forward vision—something home seekers proudly own!

In a rallying market — a constant game of chameleon shifting between "what's hot" and "what's not." Keeping fingers on the pulse means spotting upcoming real estate changes before they hit. Staying prepared for another turnaround.

Market Cycles: The 'Wheel of Real Estate Fortune'

To be honest, real estate is much like a wheel of fortune – it keeps spinning, and holding a finger on its pulse is a strategy chart-topper. Trace that pulse through keen market sensing and tie those with possible opportunities. Know your apples (houses), your baskets (seller's market), and stay watchful for the shells (buyer's market). Understanding these key tweaks to the real estate sphere makes navigating so much more productive and neater. Dig-out from buyer's market for future goldmines. Map ties in a seller's market for longevity and success. After all, we can impact til' we know the impression we're making, right?
Paint the market currencies—patience or strategic activeness—to best color your opportunities canvas. Remember: one doesn't drown by falling in the water; one drowns by staying there. Learn, adapt, evolve—with every real estate tide, make the markets work for you. After all, who knows your reality better than you? Let understanding the currents guide your sail, mate.

Chapter 12: Exit Strategies and Selling Rental Properties

Determining the right time to sell

Imagine it's a lovely Saturday night catch up over the barbecue, and you're dubiously gazing at your beer mug, contemplating your bundle of rental properties. Questions like "Should we sell?", "How do we know it's the right time to sell?" bounce in your mind. Let's get deep into the thick of it and scrape your dilemma with a crisp lens.

Exit Strategies 101

Alright now, let's start with the nuts and bolts. Exit strategy? Sounds complicated, right? Not to worry. All it means is your game plan to sell your properties to maximize return on investment (ROI), or simply put more cash in your pocket. Think of it as your "out" plan when you think enough money has been made – or to cut down any potential losses. Exit strategies are like satellite navigation techniques. There are many ways to reach your destination (The "EXIT" sign!), each with its distinctive mixes of yields, efforts, drawbacks, etc.

Every savvy real estate investor, just like you buddy, must go into a venture with an eye, not just on nifty profit opportunities of the 'now', but also on beneficial prospects after the time to skim off comes.

So, why do you need an exit strategy?

Imagine buying a classic car in mint condition. Smells sweet, huh? Now imagine having limited ways of selling it after you're done enjoying the ride. Not so delightful, is it? Having a decent exit strategy means turning those dollars to dimes based on anticipated changes in your investment; seasonal, cyclical or definitely when they start drearily bleeding cash!

Having a robust exit strategy can prevent panic in uncertain times, provides liquidity when you need it, plays a massive role to chalk how to minimize taxes, and reduces the overall risk profile of your real estate investing career. Let's say it creates a nice-crisp end goal that makes navigation through the real estate soiree, sweet and frankly, a tad bit sensible.

Deciding to Sell: factors to consider

We're easing into it, no pressure. There are several vital factors when calling the cards on this play:

The market: Look for signs the market is cooling - a slump in house prices or lack-of-bid wars. Dropping rents are also tell-tale signs.

deteriorating neighborhoods : Have crime rates shot up? Uncollected bunch of garbage? Deteriorating public stats- schools, transport services? Ain't so great for value! Probably best to cash-out.

Too much effort: Over-demanding renters, exhausting maintenance, obnoxious management or a tougher pandemic- induced operating environment - maybe it's time to rethink?

Needing cash reserves: if other investments are more tempting or you urgently need liquidity- home improvement, kids' education, secure retirement

Changes in financial ambition or personal circumstances

Spend some time analyzing each variable, chat with peer investors, probe local property clubs, consult with your financial advisor- perspective helps!

Timing your sale - sometimes there's an apparent rationale. Technically, "When to sell?" should resonate with, "When, can you make the most money?" Obvious. Let's divide it down:

Wait for cash-before-tax income after considering an extensive range of properties values. Key upcoming economic factors might push property prices south.

You will be charting annual rental views for your property. Conservatively seek out pricy-rental zones on the increasing curve, punch in those rents and realize- AHA! Time to sell!

Look at cash-after-tax proceeds, calculate the broad risk-adjusted net present value. Does that fetch garnished returns if you pooled into more minor loans carried over due acquisitions that can sell off serenely? There's the cherry!

Essentially what I'm saying fellow advocate, is:" Are you making less than what stellar real estate benchmarks track? " Sweet barbequed hassle-free bills speak volumes. Usually.

The silent horse to note here pal, is the omnipotent "tax". It could assume unprecedented shapes- capital gains (current holding >12m), Depreciation Recapture Tax, 1031 Exchange related theories, primary residence exclusions- the tax devil lurks! And loud. Proceed bare, diligent eyes fully glued to its impact and robust tax-advantaged techniques.

Ready to Let Go of the Landlord Life?

Have you scaled the mountains of becoming a property investor, only to find the valleys on the other hand a wee bit obscure? Trust me, I've been there. You and I, we've put our blood, sweat, and probably more tears than we'd like to admit, into our lovely rental properties, subsequently to grow our wealth. But now, finding ourselves at the crossroads and deliberating to mug up on exit strategies and selling our dear rental properties, where do we start, huh? So let's park up here for a minute, my friend, grab a cuppa, and explore together the simmering process of preparing the rental property for sale.

Are we on the same page?

Very first things paramount; are you really into selling the rental property? Whenever we talk about prepping up the property for market, let's not kid - it can hardly be deemed as a walk in the park. Be dead cert about this being the most suitable exit strategy, given your financial considerations, portfolio outlook and the ilk. There are certainly alternative strategies - refinancing or bringing in an equity partner for instance.

If on firm ground to say goodbye to your landlord lives, jobs a good'un and let's buckle down.

Sec is Your Inspection Checklist Large?

Wow, haven't we seen the gruesome instances when people scorn the very first step and, to their horror, a shunned catacomb hit back ponderously? Days off-market during the last-minute frenzied patch-ups make a sizeable effigy set to flame. Rather than skipping headily to swell marketing advice by Tommy, try wooing Mrs. Attention to Detail. Inspecting the property is downright indispensable. Check for plumbing hassles, electricity problems, outdated fixtures, carpet refurbishment, gardening troubles and you can literally make the longest checklists if needed.

If that irks your comfort quo, consider forking out for a professional inspection – you can hardly regret shooting for short pay occasionally.

Repairing on a Shoestring: Your Survival Guide

That's right, I'm sensing an audible gulp down there. Repair work might be a bit rough, also biting some 'wee' chunk down your profits (seriously a sweet euphemism, right?). Now wearing the frugality hat and aiming at fixing things rather than going for overkills, sounds terrific on papers. Do address major problems like burst pipes, broken fixtures, electrical rawness and the unpleasant finishes. Dripping faucets and shaky door handles, now that's serious business. The devil, acting like a child, is sure to be hiding in details. Where are the colossal return generators, I hear you ask. Focus on kitchen, bathroom, paint jobs and at a relatively cheaper scale, lighting, trust me on helping bag silk purses even from the sow's ears. Use the wholesaler, loved the discounted refurbishments? More than you can imagine! And don't run scared, with thriving repair YouTube tutorials, this battle, my brave-hearted champions, has got us in all good places without losing a clamp-jawed bishop.

Setting Stage with Flair

Ask seasoned sellers, should it look like living or veer towards stale? Simple, say cheese as you live instead of choky cheesiness. But true, cheesy metaphor parlance class for another day. Excuse me slipping into… but I hope you grabbed the direction. Don't leave the property empty - there's a dire need balancing the sterile look sternly marketed properties occasionally brag.

Professionally staging inside: is a swell guest allowed to have sleepy looks? Jokes apart, some cost-effective, lightweight furniture props are spinning lovely yarns about looks. Remember that small-slung attitude expressed visually does jack the buyer souls ready to be devoured fondly. Outdoor work isn't to be dunked! Use some accessible landscaping, positively affecting prospect's decision-making capabilities. With an exalted spirit, rake up those first impressions, my mates.

Upload crisp, professional photos, virtual tours; lemon verbena can fondly smack onto senses. Why not use additional sales points, freshly installed garden decks or safe garbage disposals to pip the offer chances. Devote sufficient effort you see; love letters usually receive the fond replies
(I mean the glossy property packages or best marketing directions embodying pronounced features).

Pricing, at the End of It All

Honestly, we have squirrelled along quite a lot already right. But setting the right price, my friends, warrants a separate dedicated tea house talk (bitter doesn't make a credible demonstration though!). Navigate the pendulum swing skillfully, using your real: imagined price ratio. How to obtain an existing grasp over local ricing inferences or professional aid at your gate for an authoritative property appraisal? On a beneficial feature survey or asking help from other property investors in town, the options are well endowed: similar as the polite inquiry that never broke the nostrils. Right then pals, I reckon we've chewed the fat wholesale over the pioneering process, preparatory steps to sling the gemstones well. Therein lies the confident embarking ceremonies or that fun-loving first date in readiness. Blighty speaks affectionately such emotional vibes we intertwine unsuspectingly. That simpering potential buyer, irked landlords, assertive tenants, pugnacious agents and then we, frazzled yet hopping and whistling spectacularly. Isn't selling properties akin charming playing partners in diversified marks underspecified yet? Long and the short hauls swaying nearly and as every waking golden vista (shaken off colourful sheds-built roving): we find ourselves always and thankfully ready, isn't it all marvelous in nit? That clinch, err no-pinch phase represents frantically charged engaging rewards.

Marketing the property effectively

Picture if you will be owning multiple rental properties, happily managing tenants and realizing decent monthly earnings. But there comes a certain time when, for various reasons, you realize you're up for a bit of a change. Don't worry—it is not only you that faces this situation, almost all property landlords are back and forth on exit strategies and selling rental property at some point. Gladly, I present some wisdom nuggets about how to market your property, drawn from personal experiences and seasoned peers in the industry.

Getting started: There's no magical one-size-fits-all plan on marketing properties because every sale context is quite different. For instance, probably the two scenarios maybe sale by compulsion due to economic pressures while there is also the strategic sale to maybe reinvest or switch investment to a more beneficial venture. In both axes, a calculated sales strategy certainly boosts your chances to land the killer deal.

So, what are some potent marketing strategies to offer your rental property?

Pass-a-glower Photo Prowess

Photos are highly instrumental in expanding your exposure, and every added online presentation reduces the selling-intro gap. But don't stop at the number of pictures; capitalize on capturing high-quality exciting images that excite viewers and portray your property in the best light possible—you'd attain brilliant results. These visuals communicate the farthest amid a masses brush on the sight for commodities online or offline. Indeed, it's common that people raise viewing attempts better on space-detail pictures for any fixed-price item of a catalog—you'd affirm this, yes?

A Big Catch in Accurate Pricing

There's reasonable confusion when pinning an accurate price on why there are estimates of selling assets in real estate. An overpriced property interprets dim, lingering shadows of anguish, counting strayed valuable time in property investors' chronicle. Here's the deal—fewer buyers are keen enough to pry into extravagantly labeled properties with the limelight on other probably fairly priced options readily available strutting the marketplace—yet there are pros to play the card here decently getting you winning.

Essentially, always adopt comparative property monitoring—pinpoint the other rentals in near field/size/niche and count off either favorably to your advantage. It gives leeway to buyers and portrays you as a tuned-in seller, deliciously nurturing towards closing a deal. This move equally corrects the risk of an underpriced property, which draws bidders very swiftly but leaves you counting lower earnings in a decent tide.

Job Cutout in Legalities

You might want to solicit professional advice against confused jabs here and there if, for instance, easements, encroachments, property line issues, or more sophisticated layers like unpermitted improvements notoriously line your sale. Ignoring legal limitations can circle back at you in horrific lawsuits or slower sales circumstances due to an opaque disposition—there's a lot not appealing in this.

An Investment in a Good Condition Charm

From landscaping a fantastic view on the exterior, simplifying furniture organizing in the interior, up to combed cleaning cues striking right into staging the property, capitalizing on broadcast-ready characters will spruce every potential buyer's aura uplifting the selling curtain. A well-showcased property will immediately look more attractive to potential buyers, increasing your chances of a productive sale. Keep your property pristine!

Establish Healthy Relationships with Tenants

Ally on your on-board tenants if there be. You'd perform terribly with snubbed anchors when tenants innocently crop land a bit scary gossip of the marketing attempt from the grapevine. Do everything you can to ensure that your tenants feel as comfortable as possible during the transitional period—not excluding possible place shifts. Bare this king-black swan in consideration when leaning for sales, how about monthly perks, a deserved discount, or carving out decent time for property viewing sure to keep you away from beatings and slump investments—it guarantees swift passage through the market radar.

In conclusion, never take off on your waiting hat too pleasingly. Brilliant sales hardly peek up in everybody's flashy marketing—doesn't exactly mean a hesitated calamity befell your clean plate.

Optimizing and refining your marketing funnel is an iterating experience incredibly paying to tenacious fellows. A rightly cast net maintains chances atop playful tides and adapts smoky pressures out with irresistible efforts easily booked attempts.

In short, a well-packed marketing approach means loads of accolades. Draw in your strategic sales, keep your exit angles spacious, less haunted by troublesome experiences. It intricately decorates a welcoming system of rental properties' profitability even as customers brilliantly spot cues clever-yielding delicious favors upon your spread anchor.

Negotiating and closing the sale

I thought I would share some insight on a gripping topic: exit strategies and selling rental properties. It's a big decision, you might be thinking, "Where do I begin?" or "What negotiation tactics should I apply?". The forthcoming exhilarating moments will broaden your knowledge about negotiations and the completion of rental property sales.

Starting Right: The Exit Strategy

Getting out on the right foot plays a crucial part, and that's where an exit strategy comes into play. Now, you might ask, "Wait, what is an 'exit strategy?'"

An exit strategy, friend, simply involves planning how to sell or otherwise "exit" an investment, which in our case, is the rental properties. So why is it needed, you ask? The reason is pretty simple; having an exit strategy reduces uncertainty and risks and prepares you for when things might not go as planned.

Understanding What You Want: The Goals

Like any negotiation or decision in life, understanding what you want out of the sales process is crucial as it sets the ground rules for the terms, prices, and conditions. Consequently, you'll get an idea of whether the price offered matches your expectations and enables you to prepare your negotiation tactics.

Negotiate Like A Pro

Remember negotiations as kids when you wanted the last piece of the pie? Some of those methods - minus the whining, emotions, and screaming - can be put into great use during negotiations of this scale.

Knowing Market Values Are Key

Knowledge gives you power in negotiations. Be conversant with the rental market, get estimates of recent real estate sales, and consider factors like neighborhood, availability of amenities et cetera —equated to draw the best price for you.

Empathy Matters. But It's Business!

It's easy to immerse ourselves in negotiations ruthlessly. Sometimes, we might even be high on emotions, especially if the property's been lived, vibe, breathed in. However, keeping in time, effort and compliance into account, ensure not to undersell. Fact: Everybody wants a good deal, not selling efficiently can result in delayed income from property.

Letters of Intent

Once negotiations start on a promising note, follow this up with a Letter of Intent - a smart document that states the price, earnest money amount, due diligence period, and other significant terms. Here's a Pro tip, friend: Remember, a Letter of Intent isn't legally binding; it's more of a promising "in good faith" step for you and the buyer.

Details often get juggled in transcribing. Practise a wide-angle eye for detail. Specifically, check pre-established fees as part of contractual conditions can really substitute down profits.

Closing the Sale

Firstly, huge congratulations! Once your agreement seems palpable enough, your close lies just some steps away under the right conditions and paperwork. Here's what final thrill lurks -

Due Diligence

Once you've caught the potential buyer's eye, due diligence follows suit. This is where a thorough inspection of your property and all its documents happens.

Do remember, once real owners come into conduct their inspections, keep everything neatly arranged. Selling works more effectively when buyers are mind-passported a clean visual of your space!

Chapter 13: Case Studies and Success Stories

Real-life examples of successful rental property investments

You know, there's something I've wanted to talk to you about for a while now. We've talked about investments, and you've shown a great deal of interest especially in rental property investments. I thought I'd share some case studies and success stories with you. This way you could take a much closer peek at what it all really means before diving in yourself. Let's get started, shall we?

Case Study 1: Conversion Strategy

Let's go check out our first case study. Say hello to Anna's real-life example.

Anna is a simple hardworking professional like us who wanted to grow her nest egg. She was particularly attracted to multifamily homes. You might wonder why 'multi'. It's simple! Multifamily homes are known to gain value faster than single-family houses - Alot of potential for bigger returns! Not to mention the fact that if one unit is vacant, she'd still have other inflows coming - Sound plan, right? She bought her first property, a duplex, at an auction for pennies on the dollar due to the rough condition it was in. Got it renovated using local contractors from her network, which saved tons on labor and material costs. Subsequently converting one property into two ready-to-lease units. Today, both are rented and yield substantial monthly rents! Since she lives nearby, handling day-to-day issues never seemed upsetting too. Consequently, with first property success, her confidence ended up propelling her dive into numerous others. She'd now made property investments 'literally' her full scaling earning stream. Isn't that conversion strategy a trick to reckon?

Success Story 2: Turnaround Strategy

Now my friend, turn your glance at Britney's turnaround strategy story. She's a go-getter I know who bought a foreclosed condo in a descent neighborhood that have seen escalating property prices. Her rescue mission involved gradually sprucing up the property over a span of 6 months while juggling her full-time job. Ultimately, she sought help from a property management firm, dozing off the anxiety over handling repairs and tenants issues while conforming with tenant-landlord laws {such a life-saver for working professionals, right?}. Almost needless to say, but wouldn't it be thrilling to hear, that soon the property prices soared and rewarded her enough net cash flow to support all her heart's recreational desires. More so, it also made her capable of paying off huge part of college tuition loans way earlier than she'd planned. Let alone all the rewarding experiences this property adventure reciprocated her with.

So, interesting possibility reinforcement with a property turnaround investment plan, yeah?

Success story 3: Buy-and-Hold Strategy

Introducing Ben! - retired, seasoned investor known in developing mindful of safety-net around the family through his understanding of buy-and-hold investment strategy. In '90s Ben acquired mid-sizes rental properties, pushed up their rents which he funneled to mortgage debts resulting a decade long strengthening balloon payment. As economy fluctuated, rent rates continued to increase, provided a steady cream on top. More so, now he placed the plan of passing them to next-generation; With the strings of financial security and gaining legacy present income. Landscape of property investment is rife with buy-and-hold strategy being promising and logical in many scenarios. We stumbled across some engaging facts and experiences pooling a vast range of possibilities in Rental Property Investment ocean here, didn't we mate?

We examined Anna's foresight with conversion strategy. After came Britney's fact on turning around properties. And last, Ben's long-term vision with buy-and-hold strategy; Their ingenuity with rental properties opened horizons I feel. You think recently more about investing idle cash, you think turning it fruitful with Rental properties?

Lessons learned from experienced investors

Let me tell you a story today. But hold on, let this not be your standard run-of-the-mill kind of story. This is going to be about some real high-flying wolves of Wall Street. I'm talking about experienced investors, who have smelt success in the ever-winning game of playing with stocks and assets.

Don't rule it out as dry and dull just because it contains numbers and predictions, but take it as inspirational tales teaching us valuable lessons from extraordinary people.

Case Study 1: Humble Brag about Warren Buffet

As you foray into the world of investment, one name surely crosses your path often right, Warren Buffet. No one casually amasses a fortune of $78 billion in a wildly volatile world of investment. Let me tell you a quick secret, Buffet rightfully gets his rich legend status because he ingeniously grabs the opportunities or takes strategic risk decisions that others may hesitate to try. Who would have thought that anyone would invest 40% of their funds into a Nebraskan textile company which was essentially wrong-labelled from being a "terrible business" to "Buffett's best investment," simply because he figured its capability of becoming an effective defensive-parking place for incoming cash! Isn't mind-blowing how he would take risks with an eye for long-term reward? I can confidently tell you my friend, patience is the key, well, at least one of them.

Case Study 2: Speaking Volumes for Paul Tudor Jones

Next in line is this still energetic maverick, Paul Tudor Jones, or as you might find amusing, PTJ. What sets him apart is a truly mesmerizing display of reading clues from numerous markets before deciding to invest. When most of his contemporaries distanced away from Chrysler Corp when it flirted with bankruptcy in 1980, eccentric PTJ decided to invest, not on Chrysler, but on companies supplying parts to them. PTJ's boldness might be intimidating, but his foresight proved its magic. My friend, an essential lesson for you is to reimagine risk-taking with proper research and analysis, that too, beyond immediate investment options. Not all of your odds will shine, but it surely increases your chances of winning.

Case Study 3: Raving about Ray Dalio

Last, but not least is Ray Dalio, widely recognized for the use of his serene methodical approach. As another analogy, tune back to his stagflation bets in 1971. Credit is kept at minimal levels and most investment or forecasts were relatively safe. Friends, tuning to macro factors is like playing the supporting cast for your already brilliant portfolio. But don't just let your guards down with every successful streak, remember all these brilliant investors weren't always winning!

Success Story: Jim Simons, the Coding Wizard

Talking about hitting walls brings me to Jim Simons. Mathematician you said? Right but also one among the globe's best hedge fund managers. But listen to his tale! Resilience, just like the Pharaoh of Phoenix, his series of successful quant-trading starts highlight the importance of coming back from the loss, coding that resilience into blooming success! Now how about math genius when markets begin mocking numbers and traditional theorems! Generically, stop being all scared at walls; they are there for everyone. But bravely bust them as the superheroes just did, take calculated risks. Riding winning streaks, sure strike more often, but remember such monstrous hits (read dives) are inevitable.

Those boring maths classes in high school? They sure didn't warn you then.

The lessons we can take away from pro-investors

Relax there my friend, my incessant chat must be remodeled too. Let me wrench out a few key pointers before wrapping this up:

Patience Pays

Take calculated risks, pursue thorough analysis, but don't latch and pounce upon random possibilities; Remember Buffet playing the waiting game and how it paid off.

Dig Beyond the Surface

Engage clever observation like Paul, don't just leap onto usual endeavors but dig beyond into competent allies and reap profitable yields.

Analysis of Macro Factors

While we always tend to concentrate only on the investment destination, take a step back like Ray, align yourself with macroeconomic events.

Never Shy from Challenges

Freaked out? Worried? Losses at your sight? Just don't hit the "Exit" button; let resilience guide as did Jim!

Mixing math and intuition, while having a helpful black coffee (although I ought to have kept both math and coffee in surprise shells!). Joking pal, proper information, boosted by agility and garnished with immense persistence, gets them out as paradigms of experienced investors.

Analyzing different investment strategies and outcomes

There are so many success stories and case studies out there; real examples that can actually help us understand how things really work in the world of investments - from stocks to startups, from real estate to retirement funds.

I thought it would be great to dive a little deeper into some of these case studies to get a point-by-point understanding about different investment strategies – what worked, what didn't, and what we can learn from that.

So, sit tight, grab a cup of coffee and let's dig in!

Stock Market Success: The Story of Warren Buffet

You must know about Warren Buffet - the legendary share market guru. In the 1960s Buffet began buying stock in Berkshire Hathaway. He expanded the company, which was initially a textile manufacturing firm, through purchases of insurance companies and other investments. According to Forbes, as of early 2021, Buffet has a net worth of $100.4 billion. Yep, billion!
-The key takeaway? Your property is worth as much as people are willing to pay for it. Warren showed buy-and-hold might not be exciting, but it has wheeled serious wealth for those willing to stick to a plan.

Time in the Market is Better than Timing the Market: An Everyday Hero Story

Let me acquaint you with Bob - who is deemed the worst market timer in the world. Bob began investing in the late 1970s, and throughout his lifetime he only made investments at the peak of the markets and immediately before each crash. Despite all this, due to his "long-term view" and his decision to never sell, Bob's portfolio managed to grow to 3 Million by the time he retired. This story emphasizes one critical point about investment: time in the market matters more than timing the market.

Flipping the Real Estate Investment Game: The Case Study of The BRRRR Method (Buy, Rehab, Rent, Refinance, Repeat)

Let's shift the gears and talk about real estate. Are you familiar with BRRRR method? No? That's okay. BRRRR is a modern mantra among young real estate investors, and quite successful I must say! City slicker superstar, Justin reads about the desolate home prices in the heartland of USA, decides to move out from super-expensive California, moves to Ohio, and starts to buy dilapidated houses, refurbishes them and rents them for a respectable income. Once rented, he gets them refinanced so he can take out the invested capital to REPEAT the cycle. Ten houses down after 5 years, this former techie is way more secure, return on investment (ROI) beating any stock market bulls over the period! -Lessons? Big fish survive not just in big ponds! Diverse investment opportunities exist if you broaden your horizons.

Disruption Creates Opportunity: Exploring Startup Investments

Startups… the buzzword in investment trends! Let me tell you about Chris Sacca. Started out as a lawyer in Google, involved in IPO, became an Angel Investor in the greatest tech disruption wave taking advantage of the all the understanding of ecosystem to make prosperous bet. Notable ones? Twitter & Uber to name a couple! -The moral? Disruption creates immense opportunities if captured timely and with a risk appetite.

Chapter 14: Mistakes to Avoid in Rental Property Investing

Common pitfalls and mistakes to watch out for

So, you're starting to dip your feet into the muddy water of rental property investing? Awesome! There is a wealth of opportunity out there just ripe for the plucking. BUT, before you get on this roller-coaster ride, you should be aware of the 'bumps n gloom' or common hiccups that can truly slow you down or even halt your property investment journey.

Hitting the Hammer Without Set Goals

Entering the property market without set goals can be likened to embarking on a drive without a destination in mind. Yes, the journey may be eventful, but without a set goal, you'll likely just round up going in circles. Before you dive head-first into property investment, review what you want to achieve. It could be to accumulate wealth, have a passive income for retirement, or gain equity for reinvesting. And while goals may be subject to change over time, having a target gives your investment journey a clear direction.

Rocking in the Deep Without Proper Research

Friend, take it from me, there are no shortcuts on the road to prosperity. Neglecting thorough research can cost you BIG time. When it comes to rental property investing - know the market, dig the deals, find the trends. Locality plays a pivotal role in determining property values - research neighborhood amenities, crime statistics, nearby schools, and any other factors that influence real estate prices. Trust me, burying your head in these dirt heaps of data can truly save you from an investment tumbleweed later!

Dodging Pool Depth & Wading in With All Your Money

There is a reason people advocating for investing always focus on the golden rule - diversification. Placing all your hard-earned eggs in a single basket can leave you reeling if the market tanks. The world of property investing has intensively varied facets and entirely relying on one can be business suicide. Try spreading your wings around single-units, multi-units, duplex apartments, and even commercial properties for an illusion of safety net.

Siding With 'Do-It-Yourself'

Investing in rental property isn't all about shaking hands and collecting rent. Like every other sector of life, property investing flourishes where there is a partnership. Surround yourself with a group of competent professionals who understand the game. Think legally (lawyers), financially (tax consultants, accountants), and physically (realtors, contractors). And while handing out these responsibilities might seem to 'dent' your wallet at first, consider the time-&-stress-saves which literally translate to dollar-saves!

Wearing a Blindfold to The Skeletons (Hidden Costs)

Unlike mere purchasing real estate where you pay and pack your stuff to enjoy your haven, investment properties come with piles and piles of hidden costs. Property management, repairs, insurance, property tax, vacancy, not to mention possible rise in interest rates, can shake that ROI bottom if ignored. When budgeting for an investment property, always remember clouds do come with silver linings.

Belittling the Lease

Never ever underestimate the power of a perfectly nailed contract document. The least you would want is a raging tenant horror scenario, property damages, or lawsuits floating in unchartered territories. Having solid legal documentation about the lease bejewels the property and the owner with protection. Lease agreements need to outline the responsibilities of all parties involved, violation consequences, and acts as a reference point in case any misunderstanding arises.

Lessons from failed investments

Although, like any other investment playground, if you don't toe the baseline and meet your groundstrokes just right, you could end up double faulting rather spectacularly—pardon my tennis metaphors, you catch my drift though. Let's shoot the breeze about some real disasters in the rental property sphere to help you hedge bets like Warren Buffet!

Plunging in with Sketchy Research

You've heard this a thousand times, yes, yes—"Knowledge is Power". Clueless investing is somewhat like being thrown into the kitchen and expected to produce a gourmet meal without a recipe book. So, bass-ackwards, am I right?

Avoid slapping yourself with a raw deal by getting your hands-on real comps—comparable homes in the neighborhood that have been recently leased or sold. They help jot the rate charts out. Next, correlate this to typical law & regulatory tidbits, cost of living stats, gross median rent, versatility of the job market there—basically the DNA of your "market traits," if you will.

If all that sounds about as fun as watching paint dry, get a professional in your corner—you owe it to yourself to make sound business decisions! Miss this beginner step, and you become one of those classic 'penny wise, pound foolish' tales.

Ignoring Cash Flow & Cash-on-Cash Return

A seasoned player will carp, "cash is not income, but inflow." Listen up, newbie. Just stick your property on the digitized world, get your rent and smile at the bank, while forgetting about pesky goblins like repair maintenance, vacancies, property management, and even tax levies. Those dang expenses, they have a kooky knacky-noodle way of showing up at just about the same time and depleting the razzle-dazzle from your rental be dazzler!

So, measure your free and unaffectionate cash first. Then peek and take refuge in the underbelly of the 'cash-on-cash return' strategy. This simple return of investment calculation, comparing the actual cash earned to cash invested annually, can go a long way in arranging your thoughts into sequitur safety-lines.

Neglecting Quality Property Management Teams

Okay, now don't give me a flat old stare-cum-gape on this one—your 'unleashing the inner estate exec' aspiration while having an ole 9 to 5 hip shebang is a delusional parallel existence. You don't have the free rein here, cowpoke!

That means, if your faucets scream louder than a Carnyx at midnight or the kitchen cult deems it suitable for Project I'm-on-fire war movies, ignoring a professional crisp management team can trigger your primal scream. It's just like acting your own attorney in courts—you save on professional costs while generating tons of heartburn, eh?

Underestimating the Potential of Market Dip

Rome was not built in a day, and friend, neither was the courage of a property investor in a depreciating market. Picking low-priced properties isn't an invitation to the monthly downward percolating graph—akimbo all lost. It is to understand that in a recession, less is more and more is less, be brave enough to buy when most sell.

In short, it's sometimes about buying umbrellas in the sunshine, hoping for rain, dear chap until the cyclic market gears kick in the bling! Ah, brave this risk with poise and there will no stopping of that kerching-kerching.

This chapter is brilliantly titled "Mistakes to Avoid," and it's been a treasure trove of useful strategies on how to mitigate those potential investing pitfalls and risks. Grab a cup of cocoa, tea, or your preferred beverage, and let's dive right in together, like good ol' times.

Summary of the Mistake to Avoid

Rental investing, like all other forms of investment, comes with some risks you ought to consciously look out for, or you could find yourself in a pretty tough spot. Sometimes these risks translate into intimidating tax obligations, negligent tenants, or poorly chosen locations; other times, it could be unexpected vacancies reducing your income. Long story short, acknowledging these risks upfront, having a game plan, and better risk mitigation focus is imperative to staying afloat in this real estate adventure you are about to or already have ventured into!

1. Deciding to DIY your Management Tasks

Let's be real. Taking the alluring DIY route can be tricky when managing your real estate property. A proverb quoted with love in the business world stipulates "Just because you are a great cook doesn't mean you should run a diner," and no truer words have encountered mortgage repayments. Engaging the services of a trusted professional property management team can alleviate the potential direct stress and hassle that comes with rental properties.

2. Choosing a "Rushed" Location

As we always rib each other over the weekend games, haste makes waste! The same can be said of rushing into picking a location. The neighborhood makes up but one important aspect when considering new property. Look out for a balance of demographics, services, and growth potential to avoid investing in an appetizing pie you can't stomach in the market later on.

3. Slyly Underestimating Expenses

Of all surprisingly easy trapping dead-ends, underestimating your potential expenses is a doozy. From welcoming your tenants with a spruced-up place, upkeep, repairs, taxes, amongst others, the tabs can add up faster than a mystery bar tab on your bachelor's party.

4. Skipping Background Checks on Potential Tenants

Do you remember our high school drama club mate Robbie who always shared wild stories about tenants from hell? My recent mental expedition in real estate sent me clashing bumpers with that reality more times than I dare count. A quick fixes solace:

Routine background checks on prospective tenants reduce your chances of housing rental space nightmares significantly. Poor refs, credit histories, past evictions and the likes are brightly clad red flags, buddy.

5. Fancying a Gloss Over Lease Agreement

My friend, watch out for the Trap of Oversight - neglecting to run all lease agreements via an attorney's keen scanning eye because A bad agreement can land you on legally shaky grounds or leave potential loopholes that recouping tenants conveniently exploit, therefore always ensure your documents are legally tight.

Strategies to Mitigate Risk:

Alright big guy, now that we're familiar with the major traps laying in wait while navigating the rental property business highway, let's discuss crucial tactics to avoid falling into them.

For your DIY Management Aspirations:

It would be telling your investment squad where secret aces are located on the deck to say you necessarily need to toss every DIY aspect of managing on the trash heap. Instead, focus on creating an emergency checklist highlighting key potential problems and how they should be handled so that direct professional help would come in handy for more complex issues.

Choosing a Positive Rental Property Location

Roll your investment/ job/business/prospecting/economic/geographical/gut instincts into one and seeing the availability and pricing for many types of properties in different locales currently on-wheels would help determine a realistic rental pricing model for potential property purchases you may be considering. Allow balance guide your calculations.

Making Room for Exiting on the Right Investing Side:

Despite your calculated engagement, bear in mind that things could unexpectedly turn sour – it's part of life's tangy taste basket we occasionally have to chow on. Therefore, entering every investment with an exit strategy would make proverbial idealness seem plausible. Choose investments with multiple strategies in case rent does not show the expected increase, or sales fall does short outcome marks.

Keeping a Protecting Hitman:

Keep this between you and me, okay? Where your properties located (state/city/township/county), is interested in collecting property taxes off rental income. Don't be slugged by surprise tax punches from your friendly government reps. Become really best friends with your tax attorney.

Chapter 15: Building a Network and Resources

Networking with real estate professionals

Let's grab a coffee e-friend and discover the impressively vast world of networking in real estate. Because believe me, relationships are basically worth their weight in gold!

The Importance of Networking in Real Estate

First off, you've gotta realize one thing - the engine that runs the real estate business isn't properties, but people! The potential to adequately understand, persuade, and motivate them can make or break your venture. This is what you get when you're building your network. So, how does networking come in? Simply put, when you network with the right folks, your pool of potential deals, sales, partnerships, knowledge centres, and other real estate opportunities go up significantly. Easy to comprehend, right?! In real estate, the capacity to effectively network isn't just a plus. Nah-uh… it's literally a prerequisite. So, building a booming estate empire that fills up your pocket and saturates those business goals is almost impossible without establishing those meaningful connections.

Let's delve a bit deeper together.

Who Are These Real Estate Professionals?

Alright, as much as Emma Stone captured my heart in 'The Amazing Spider-man', "with great power, comes great responsibility"; once you understand why you need to network, it's equally critical to identify these potential mentors and partners. Let's explore the realm of real estate professionals together. Real estate agents: You have the agent-legends who have been mingling with listings for God knows how long. They live and breathe the real estate industry day-to-day and can guide your moves. Agents naturally link up with both local and cross-country clients, lenders, contractors, and whatnot - pretty much covering buyer education, strategic tactics, payment supervision, and more. Lenders: Got to get cash flow for any trades? Lenders help ease up the financial constraints and sometimes might even be willing to offer a flexible rate for impressive ideas the debtor offers.

Contractors: Your contractors' team will literally revamp your transitional properties and potentially help you sell and rent out better.

Real Estate Attorney: When it comes to drafting agreements with sellers or buyers, advice on unforeseen market scenarios, you cannot quickly get help unless you know a real estate attorney.

Investing Partners or groups: Do I even have to explain how paramount these individuals are for pouring in funds or advice on real estate moves?!

You still with me bud? Too much information to take in? Guess that comes when we're talking about something this significant!

Techniques to Build a Powerful Network

Apart from being a buoyant socializer who loves spending time with people, what are other tricks in the bag to build impressive links in the estate kingdom?

Virtual Networking: Social Media and real estate apps like BiggerPockets, Meetup, LinkedIn are steeping in advice blogs, and let one connect with mentors just with a click. They function somewhat like mastermind groups who would test new strategies with you before investing a penny.

Join Local Investor Clubs: Establish an understanding with these local clubs offers benefiting scenarios where the veterans share their local insights, sometimes exposing you to deals unnoticed.

Real Estate Seminars and Expos: Grab your coats and lock your meetings with expos showcasing property brands, handy ROI strategies, potential sellers, updates on goods, and more!

Customer Experience: Your first impression potentially defines your relationship timeline. Map out a welcoming email model, provide add-on services after your collaborations, and prioritize customer service!

Joining investor groups and associations

Since I started my journey as an investor a couple year back, I've realized many incredible things, one of which is— you cannot underestimate the value of YOUR network. That's right. Who you know and communicate with matters—a lot. So today I'm going to share with you how building a network and resources, especially by joining investor groups and associations, can make a substantial difference to your investing journey. Buckle up!

Why Network Matters?

Remember when you first started and you didn't have the foggiest idea the processes and rules set up by SEC for foreign investors operating in U.S markets, or the difference between Private Equity and Venture Capital? I sure do. One of the main areas where you can leverage a strong network is when you're starting. In the game of investing, much like many other fields, knowledge is power. Gaining insights, tips, and experiences directly from people who have 'been there, done that' offers an edge you would definitely want. Alternatively, maybe you've already donned your investing hat for a while, comfortably recognized investing terms, adroitness with the legal rules associated with investing, and plenty of lessons learned along the way—yet okay, why exactly would you need a network? Here is the definitive question my friend, have you ever found yourself in a situation where you had capital just waiting to be invested in an amazing opportunity but you just couldn't seem to find one? We've all been there. By having a network, specifically by being a part of investor groups and associations, you gain access to a plethora of investment opportunities that you might never have heard about—third-party investing anyone?

Investor Groups: In Perspective

Just landed your eyes on an investment opportunity and want some opinions on it? These groups are hot houses for receiving feedback. Maybe you'd get an extra layer of due diligence— a catch or detail that might whistle past you.

Aforementioned clears on how investor clubs can offer investment opportunity leads and constructive criticism, but a subtler yet equally essential reason would be access to seasoned investors and their experience. What's considerable here is not just referrals or capital injection—It's their experience, insights they've garnered from the successes and the not-so-pretty part of their careers. Equally essential? Your potential associate is probably mingling right there in the next meet.

Key examples of such networks are Real Estate Investment Associations (REIAs) and Angel Investor Groups. Locating and joining an investor network isn't particularly trouble. An internet search could get you a list within your locality. Websites like Acgroups.com and Meetup are also frequented by these groups.

Investing Associations: Who? What? How?

Now, besides these formal and not-so-formal groups, there are 'Investor Associations'. Depicting in the most straightforward form, these associations seek to promote the interests, rights, and profile of investors globally. Drawing from the best parts of your local Christmas club and the college debate team, here you can engage, an overhaul of ideas, creating camaraderie based of shared interests and missions. Notably, investing associations like NAREIT for Real Estate have the dual aim to educate and open up a communicative platform not just among investors but also conglomerates, managers, and academics. New players in hunting industries like clean-energy, booming tech start-up scene, then there are organizations like EREITs (Energy REITs) and National Venture Capital Associations manifesting platforms shared by not just the start-ups but also for fair-size fish.

You'd be amazed to see how noticeably a prolific network may impact you as an investor. They streamline what is coming—a likely drift in the legislation, new investment opportunities, last-hour trend turnarounds. In essence, joining investor groups and associations, offer not just network expansion, but deeper knowledge pools, act as places where you could potentially meet a mentor from an experienced investor just hanging around the corner.

Join in and Count on

The essence here my friend, remember to collect allies, not cards. Listen more, talk relevant. Investing-like-networking shouldn't be unilateral but bilateral medium of transaction between benefits and information. It's definitely no dirt lesson hearing up pros like Warren Buffet bespeaking "You only find out who is swimming naked when the tide goes out," whoa, remember, your goal here isn't being in the race of downing cards. May that be sheer industry knowledge or avail opportunities surfing waves hard to be flagged', you could seek assurance in knowledge of having 'built that building part right' not entirely leaving it on just theory classes and losing after sun. Join a happy-hour gathering or be an ESOP conference dude, be in the loop, but remember, JOIN IN.

Suit where it aligns, sometimes counting on a hundred relationships may expedite more dependable results than attempting on thousands. That's the magical ratio right there.

A mere alumnus social gathering extended invitation could provide new insights or finding the next high-rising fidget—bearing fruits of your investment. Yet, found yourself stranded as an investor longing for a herd or guru? 'Join a legit investing group already!' There you are ushering your new phase of exclusives' hall featuring monetary decisions becoming wisest you did. So, find a group, hop into some investor association meetings, maybe try a convention or two—and remember, we're all still learning, isn't that investing virtues after all?

And before wrapping, one hood counsel. Welcome and host every serendipity, refigure out opportunity to evolve by ultimately getting involved and make smart investments, just smarter choices, isn't that you're already oriented for?

Utilizing online resources and platforms for research and support

I've been thinking a lot lately about how important building a network and resources is for both personal and professional growth. You know, in this technological era, the whole world is technically at our fingertips. When you genuinely reflect on it, it's quite astonishing. So, let's chat through some thoughts on how we can utilize online resources and platforms both for conducting research and finding support.

Build Networks on Social Media

Firstly, let's talk about social media. Now, I know, social media has its positives and negatives, but there's no doubting the power it has when it comes to connecting with people and reaching out to a wider audience:

Social media platforms such as Facebook, Twitter, LinkedIn, and Instagram provide fantastic opportunities to interact with others professionally and to build beneficial relationships. For instance, on LinkedIn, you can easily connect with colleagues, employers, professionals from your field, or mentors. I've found it incredibly useful for professional networking.

Then you have Facebook groups which are full of individuals who share common interests, making them ideal for getting support or advice on a variety of topics.

Use Online Forums

Following that, online forums and discussions boards represent another excellent way to do this. Platforms such as Quora, Reddit, Google Groups, and specialized forums related to your professional field present exceptionally rich sources of information. Not to mention, these are places where you can exchange ideas, ask direct questions, get advice, or even provide insight to others based on your knowledge and experiences.

Blogging and Sharing Content

Blogging is another excellent way to build networks and resources. Lots of individuals, professionals, and companies use blogs like Medium or WordPress to express their thoughts, share their expertise and encourage conversation around various topics. By contributing with your own content or providing useful comments on other people's blogs, you can become part of an online community related to your field of interest.

Utilising Professional Databases

Have I mentioned online databases? Universities, research institutions, libraries, and organizations provide access to database services filled with reliable resources directly related to your studies or professional projects. Databases like JSTOR, ScienceDirect, ProQuest, Google Scholar, and others can be incredibly useful tools when it comes to serious scholarly research.

Leverage Online Tools

Furthermore, there are a handful of online tools - such as Google Docs, SlideShare, Onedrive, and Dropbox amongst others - which are not only great for storing your studies and work online but also promote collaborative work by allowing files to be accessed and updated by different users in real time.

So, navigating all this online networking and resource-finding can seem daunting, a bit overwhelming even, but it's worth the effort. This is the main act in building solid networks and finding a wealth of resources that can significantly enhance your personal learning, development, or success at work.

Everyone starts somewhere, so don't stress too much about it. Begin by exploring sites and resources that are relevant to you and make you feel comfortable. The beauty of the internet is that you can jump and dive deep whenever and wherever you're ready. Anyway, nothing can replace a good, old-fashioned in-person networking, the handshakes, the smiles, real talks (remember those?), but at least virtual networking helps in connecting us all, keeps our conversations flowing, and learning from each, no matter how far apart we are. It's a holistic approach that combines the virtual and the physical.

Chapter 16: Real Estate Market Forecasting and Analysis

Techniques for analyzing market trends

Hold on before you grab the remote and dive into today's Netflix marathon. Have you by any chance have considered investing some hard-earned dollars into real estate? If yes, welcome aboard. If no, don't silently sneak away just yet! Either way, I'd love to have a quick chat with you about Real Estate Market Forecasting and Analysis.

Ready? Ok then. Buckle up!

It may sound a bit complex – trust me - with a bit of knowledge, practice, and a healthy dollop of patience, real estate market forecasting and analysis could be much easier.

So What's This Thing Called Real Estate Forecasting?

Nope, forecasting isn't about predicting the amount of precipitation for your next beach hangout, my paranoid friend! It's all about foreseeing (or trying to, at least) the likely ups and downs in the real estate market. For instance, think about the questions: Will home prices in town X be more expensive next year? Or, is it a good time to sell off your inherited seaside condo? Answering these questions involves digging deep into multiple things: historical data, market trends, environmental factors, economic indicators and demographics to name just a few. We examine these elements to make predictions about the future of the property market.

Pulling Back the Curtains on Analysis Techniques

Different methods are deployed to analyze real estate market data and mark out trends. Here's few techniques most worth your time.

Trend Analysis

Let's start with a simple tried-and-true method: Trend Analysis. This involves examining historical property market data over a set period to spot patterns or trends. For example, if house prices have increased consistently each spring for the past five years, you could reasonably assume this upward tick might continue in the upcoming year. However, remember our friend Murphy and his law? Yep, because of this cheeky life philosophy, past patterns may not always hold for the future. So, trend analysis should only be one ingredient in your forecasting stew.

Comparative Market Analysis (CMA)

Next up is the Comparative Market Analysis (CMA).
Sounds like a Mortal Kombat style finisher, huh?
This technique boils down to comparing similar properties within the same market to get a feel for pricing trends. This method generally comes into play when selling or buying a property. Your real estate agent uses this approach to price your asset adequately.

A CMA would either use recently sold similar properties as comparisons (comparable), properties that are currently on the market, or both. Any distinctive features of the property in question (like your amazing vintage vinyl record collection or a perpetually shiny marble bathroom with a mammoth tub) are factors when cuffing together the CMA.

While CMA offers an in-depth perspective on local and property-specific details, it accompanies inherent limitations. It often doesn't have a longitudinal scope and might miss out on identifying early trend shifts.

Economic Base Analysis

Here, we get a bit into economics-over-tea talk. Force-feed yourself this if you want to seriously understand the market at a broader level. Basically, economic base analysis uses job market dynamics to predict property market trends.

Ready for a tiny step inside the cave of economics? If the local economy adds jobs faster than the population grows, property prices are pressed upwards. If the reverse is true, the pressure machine gears down. Of course, it's not so black-and-white. The type of job and the target audience also matters. Like, highly compensated tech jobs would have a different impact on property demands than low-paying service jobs.

Market Segmentation

Last but not least on our list is Market Segmentation. This technique follows the mantra that one size doesn't fit all. It helps you understand specific niches in detail. Think small – getting to know specific neighborhoods or unique property types. By familiarizing yourself with unique policies, geographies or consumer preferences associated with segments that interest you, you could emerge as a golden goose in that niche.

And There It Is!

Teamwork! Yes, you should combine these tools—together, they tell a more complete story and mitigate individual limitations of each tool. Now you can finally unwrap yourself from those fancy business news terminologies! Being an informed investor doesn't mean you must glue yourself to those yawny news channels 24/7.

Just always remember that while your bag of analysis tools gives you an edge, there's always a line between well-informed investment and future-gazing crystal gazing. Carefully balanced, real estate investment could be like that Thursday night's alfredo pasta with just the right mix of cream. Pile on too much of anything, and you are left with a wavy bowel motion later—the tycon's equivalent of capital loss!

Understanding economic indicators and factors affecting the market

Foremost, let's delve into a clear understanding of economic indicators and other impacting dynamics that are undeniably crucial in your leap into the property market. Property market forecasting isn't purely Rocket Science; it's also immensely about rational observation of all our socio-economic markers, providing a brave-new way of quantifying investing decisions.

The Handshake with Economic Indicators

Economic indicators sound absolutely like behemothic economics scholar language, right? Trust me buddy, they're just spice-n-everything-nice for our real estate discussions. At the loosest sense, these indicators perceive systematic health for an economy, via numbers tying onto parameters like production, sentiment, employment, et al. Consequently, this numerical voodoo can shed some light on expected movements maneuvered by our property thermometer, thereby sketching out real estate market forecasts. I hope we've got a basic understanding nailed here.

The most influencing indicators? Primarily the likes of GDP (Gross Domestic Product), unemployment rate, inflation, bond yields, and interest rates. When GDP shows signs of solid black coffee stimulating could mean property prices aiming for the clouds, while feelings of decaf in economic activity would arch property prices – principally of commerce-oriented establishments - plummeting. Unemployment rates behave like pesky telemarketer calls – more of these we get, expect the phone not to ring as often for the realtor standing by.

In simple words, economic indicators generally stand us in good stead to wind the hidden mechanisms that churn real estate scenarios, direct or indirectly sketchy.

Factors Influencing the Market Puzzle

As we game on through this advancing yarn, you'd probably want me to pin-point specific influencing elements in the realty market, alongside mere 'economics'. Sure, because while macroeconomic acts do hold enough aces up its sleeve, the aspect of neighborhood analysis attends the party loud and clear.

Local Amenities & Infrastructure

The adage for real estate was, is, and will be 'location-location-location', my friend. Mere steps to great schools, vicinity to vibrant shopping districts, fine medication facilities et al do significantly direct your property's compass. After all, better the neighborhood, pricier the realty leisure.

Demographics

A flash point too often failing to light is the magic sparked by Demographics. If your target region has been crumbling-aged with a younger march lining property buying spree, anticipate a jolt up the positive curve in those markets.

Government Tools - Business Zones, Rezoning and Regulation

Government intervention sizeably extends to controlling property market keys itself. Special tax breaks, business improvements districts to new zoning rules could present opportunity landmines for you to scoop up every bit the price escalation trail.

Supply & Demand Duality

If you picture property market in commerce binaries of simple supply-demand handshake, utmost enlightenment will find you ashore. If the outflow of houses is compact with relatively more punters delving for fewer bricks, then viola - we're ushering a 'sellers' market' basking prices towards a simple bullish intent.

Interest Rates

They extend on mortgage rates directly tackling our capable prize buy. Increasing interest inclines wrap us lenders inclined with caution subscribing barely lesser property geeks in the mortgage circuit race thereby strolling price narrative -

Are all these factors beginning to connect as we determine leaps and troughs of a desired property value trail? Should do, because this clarity note is certainly essential for wading past the elementary buy-to-sell objective into unseen intrinsic channels around property investment.

Let's chat a bit about an interesting topic – real estate market forecasting and analysis. It somewhat feels magical predicting the future, isn't it? Picture this – you've got a crystal ball that tells you what properties are prime for investment next year or forecasts if the market is going to skyrocket or tank! Okay, granted, it's not exactly like fortune-telling, but the concept is scarily close when it comes down to the sophisticated methods that economists and investors are using to forecast the real estate market's conditions. Fascinating, right?

Warming Up: Market Forecasting in a Nutshell

So, let's get our hands dirty. But before that, it's useful to clarify what we're precisely dealing with here. You should know that the real estate market is governed by many factors such as interest rates, the economy's health, consumer confidence, etc. Because of these various influencing factors, forecasting real estate trends might seem like a Herculean task or akin to hitting a pinpointed target with a dart… while blindfolded. Apart from luck, this surely necessitates solid analytical skills.

And ever wonder what gives this real estate forecasting a kick? Well, correct predictions can lead to significant successes, like acquiring an enormously fruitful land investment or saving the kidneys from financial loss. Conversely, miscalculations can cost heaps, like a still-not-sold vintage-style condo you jokingly thought would be gone in a moment.

See, why forecasting is paramount?

Getting Down to Business - How it's Done?

If you're like me, you would be itching to know, how is it practically done? Broadly speaking, property market watching, analyzing, and handling areas follow a reasonable stride:

Local Market evaluation — Crispy fried or donuts – unable to decide, ask locals! Similarly, to decide an investment, it's important to give due consideration to your local real estate market. At its core, forecasting is like plugging into your city's real estate gossip. You see these signs too, "House for sale!" or terrible, second-hand stories of foreclosed houses in classy neighborhoods. Field knowledge tremendously aids in elucidating local patterns leading to safer predictions.

Macro Market Analysis — You can't avoid the bigger picture—the Macro Economic data to be precise. Low interest rates, increased construction – two valuable pointers. Imagine – if after all, unemployment does soar, or if currency interest rates indeed hike, surely it would have been wise to rethink that rather perilous liaison with those sparkling new flats.

Merging of Micro-Macro understanding — This gets a little sexy. Imagine you've got local and macro-economic news straight. Now unleash the inner Data scientist in you or hire one and initiate merging subjective conversations with proven data. Voila here appeared Patterns, Trends - no spells triggering genuine insights.

Importance and Advantages

As you sip your coffee reading this, wouldn't you prefer risk likelihoods besides? It hardly feels light buying real estate property. Aiming precisely at this wager is real estate market forecasting.

Forecasting is like your stuffy buddy - sure dull and pesky at first, taking pains understanding socio-economic developments and whatnot; however once synchronize he might just secure you stuffing your giblets learning your comfy suburb is suddenly the next hip investor's hub.

Advanced analytics take forecasting way closer to an exalted science than hinging onto thin air. Like during ominous economic whirlwinds foreseeing rental income lessening or home sale rates plummeting. Early-to-bed and Early-to-rise types could complement fin dosing their elusive dreams. Avoiding significant horrid misses and grasping numerous hits rather. Why assume being shy, be sure and loud with decisions - thanks to Advancements and Forecasting!

Chapter 17: Financing Strategies for Expansion and Growth

Leveraging equity and refinancing options

The customers love your stuff and they're all over you, wanting more of the excellent product or service you provide. Happy days ahead, right? Well, sorta. Growing a business can be complicated and time-consuming in initially. Bare with me, I'm going to go over some tips on financing strategies for expansion and growth - leveraging equity and refinancing options. Hang tight, 'coz there's loads to digest here.

1. Using Equity to Finance Business Expansion

First up, the topic of equity financing. Equity is the ownership interest in your business. You can deeply leverage equity as a tool to fuel your business growth by selling a percentage of your business ownership to finance that job [*sweet!*. But how does it work fundamentally?

When you walk the equity financing path, you raise funds by offering a piece of your business - stocks - in return for cash. Depending on how much ownership you allocate to the investor - they might be able to make decisions about its running. Considering this funding boss move, inherently grants you access to potentially large volumes of cash, and interestingly you might not give a hang for immediate repayments or high interest rates. It appears to be the dream huh, but remember it also means parting ways with some degree of control over your business, which comes with implications.

What's more, raising capital via equity traditionally involves extensive legal processes and listing on public markets - thus comes with a set of underlying corporate governance responsibilities. Nonetheless, some founders are also known to "bootstrap" a business or to forgo traditional equity financing and rather use their funds. Each method has its upside and strength.

2. Deploying Debt Financing for Growth

Let's step into the unevitable territory of debt financing - a royal pathway that calls you to borrow money to ignite business flames with future repayments.

In simpler terms - debt financing strictly includes either taking out a loan or issuing a bond. When you pick a ring from debt financing, usually you invite interest rates and strict repayment time frames. Sorry, ain't a free lunch lounge!

Believe me, pal, there's also sort of grace in this path because it allows business owners to retain complete control and ownership of their venture. As an entrepreneur, it loudly encourages you to firmly nest one essential qualification: providing your ability to demonstrate a reliable history of earnings, and correctly anticipate those blazing future returns.

To further kindle your understanding, let's skim into some common form of debt financing processes you might explore:

Business Lines of Credit: Business Lines of Credit often comes in handy when wishing for buying equipment or cover unexpected expenses. Typically, worth diving, 'Coz banks often cater lower rates than credit cards.

Bank Loans: We completely know this old   friend. A secured form of fund financing sparked for business. Here again, your interest rates are influenced by how risky your venture seem to the bank loaner.

Trade Credit: Unusually trade credits could just be literally like oxygen for a successful running business. Here, suppliers allow you flexibility by extending the credit for you pending needs.

3. Hybrid Financing Route: Merging Debt and Equity

Perhaps, as an entrepreneur, you might ball out in your own flow. Steering past the purity concepts, you might instead straddle the fence and practice using both debt and equity as a hybrid means. This hybrid capital strategy has the potential to exist as the best of both worlds. Garnering external investors may finance growth while reliance on bank loans ensures the boundaries around your power to retain ownership and control.

In conclusion buddy, deciding between debt and equity financing for growth is no strolling beach holiday. Loads depend on your overall business metrics and objectives, and ultimately the financial risks you are willing to take. Navigate those complex paths and don't shrink - it's OK to change strategies as your business evolves and matures.

Remember hey, for every potential reward, there's risk tied. When seeking funds to propel your business to the new altitudes, make sure you comprehend those principles, consult honestly with your team of financial advisers, and running your business lean, footed firmly beyond gut feelings. As a careful guardian steering his ship – mind the books with great scrutiny and celebrate knowing every little crancs about your expense trends, customers acquisition cost, and sales performance. Stay sharp my friend, and I am stoked to see your business launch up to infinite levels!

navigating those potentially complex obligations under any financing approach can be daunting and overwhelming, so tread cautiously, and if necessary, don't be afraid to lean into the expertise of mentors or advisers seasoned in the business finance domain who can counsel you through your journey. Perhaps, raising multi-sources mixture or combination capital for both operational expenses and large-assets-related costs, provides you the runway way to exercise immense purpose for your business to soar amidst the tycoons.

Using 1031 exchanges for tax advantages

As an entrepreneur, it's an experience you have to look forward to. But expanding your business is far from a solitary decision; it involves a matrix of various pathways and strategies to get there. How can one finance the expansion and growth of a business? In discussing that, let's not overlook a well-kept-secret method. Surprise, it's all about taxes! Or, to be precise, taking advantage of particular tax advantages that depend heavily on exchanging like properties in a shrewdly sneaky (but totally legal) way. Yes, we are talking about a labyrinthine aspect of our tax code, the 1031 exchange.

So, what on earth is a 1031 exchange?

That's a great question! At its core, Section 1031 of the US tax code allows you to sell an investment property and reinvest the proceeds in another property while deferring any capital gains taxes. Not only can you continue to reinvest and grow, but you can keep a larger portion of your earnings out of the taxman's pocket. Cool, eh?

Using 1031 exchanges

Essentially, entrepreneurs have found themselves sandwiched in a delightful win-win scenario with 1031 exchanges. New investment adventure while evading immediate tax obligations. There is more to it than that though. It underpins financing strategies for expansion and growth with immense flexibility. "Swap til you drop!" as tax agents drive. Swapping one property for another in an exchange doesn't cut off at any given point. But, beware! This is based even on some complicated rules to do the 1031 exchange like delaying. Ah, do remember! Even a tax postponement in a 1031 exchange is not an absolute tax negation. Sounds tragic? Not so much when you place it in context. Blending deferral benefits of a 1031 exchange, with long-term low tax rates for any delayed gains potentially delivers more bang for your investment buck.

Basically, make excellent use of 1031 but don't misunderstand its modus operandi. Increased business investment is typically correlated with more significant economic activity, and extra economic demand eventually fades into additional job opportunities. Glancing over this massive labyrinthine financial equation of 1031 exchanges might make you initially lose track of the most palpable impact; it's all about enhancing your business maneuverability. By shifting how investment gains are taxed, 1031 exchanges let investors transfer valuation from older to more productive and innovative lofts in need of further investments but are stopped by intricate upfront tax considerations.

Should your business use 1031 Exchanges?

Now for the key question: "Should your business leverage 1031 exchanges?"; The answer primarily depends on your investment status and business expansion strategies. Proceed cautiously and with a chunk full of valuable advice from business consultants because this isn't an arena to leap without appropriate and intimately sage guidance. An exchange has relatively limited time: 45 days after the previous property sale to identify a potentially fitting swap, after which you merely count two additional months to finalize the purchase. Briefly put! Sleep fast, operational faster because in 1031's, "time is justice." Further, unsurprisingly, the merchandise needs to be of the equivalent kind: "like-kind" context. Non-identical portfolios constitute distinct businesses according to the hallowed grounds of constitutional interpretations. Being perplexed?! Don't be. Venturing down the 1031 interchange pathway as a music shop owner, for example, does not permit you to trade your interest with those invested in sprouting cannabis industries.

Exploring partnerships and joint ventures

Let's talk a little bit about those big dreams you've been telling me about, you know, like how you're working on expanding your business and thinking about going full-swing into growth and your future goals. Remember, success doesn't come overnight, it takes careful strategy and consistent effort.

Planning Your Vision

First and foremost, have you really thought through your strategy for growth? Because before we start talking financing and partnerships, we need to outline the big picture. Are you planning to diversify your products or services, explore new markets, or maybe grow your industry presence and reputation? Alright, I see the gears turning already. What's also important is the timing and scale of this expansion. Might sound like a challenge but, hey, you aren't in this business for effortless sailing, right?

Injection of Capital

Expansion generally requires an injection of capital, and to facilitate this, one of the common routes that business owners consider is securing investment. But then again, securing an investor entails surrendering some equity in your business, which means you're dishing out a slice of your ownership. Yup, it's quite possible but that's where 'cautious planning' then comes into picture.

Exploring Strategic Partnerships & Joint Ventures

In order to progress further, an alternative and intriguing method for funding your expansion is to delve into partnerships and joint ventures, commonly referred to as JVs in the business world.

Perhaps you might perceive them as additional investment options? While I partially agree with your viewpoint, I would also argue that partnerships and JVs involve two businesses collaborating to achieve a shared goal, rather than solely relying on financial resources for growth. You bring in a strategic partner and suddenly, not you alone, another organization also bears critical obligation to help your business kick ass. Plus, such arrangements keeps the willful control of your enterprise intact, or at least without any unwanted intrusion.

Ahoy Partners!

So, what exactly qualifies as a 'partnership'. Well, one simple designation would be when you team up with another company for mutual benefits. It could mean sharing resources like technology, HR or covering some crafty distribution strategy. Partnership enjoys this greater leeway, being less formal than a joint venture. Think of it as having a 'pact with benefits.' Sweet, eh?

Navigating Joint Ventures

And then, there are joint ventures (a.k.a. JV's if you want to sound a bit professional around your entrepreneur friends). Here, you and other entity together undertake a particular commercial project. You see, in a JV, every party contributes its share of funds, structure, markets or resources. Being more formal than partnerships, joint ventures involve their own set of complexities, legal implication and all that.

Selecting the Right Type and Partner

Choosing between a partnership or a joint venture agreement, ultimately depends on what seems the befitting move for your organization's growth requirement. But there's more to it. You got to screen out The Right Partnership from scores out there, poking and questioning - like if such an Organization would align with your business value or how strong is their commitment edge.

Balancing Risk and Reward

None of this is to forget that both partnerships & JVs do involve their risks. Even though you bring in another establishment to share your business burdens, you are at the same time, also sharing profits with them. Not to mention the risk of disagreements about decision-making responsibility, sharing of resources or potential cultural clashes.

Chapter 18: Emerging Trends in Rental Property Investing

Short-term rentals and the rise of vacation rentals

I know you've had your eye on property investment for a while now, so I figured today might be the right time to have a frank chat about what's currently making waves in the rental property circuit. Yes, my friend, before you even think of venturing into this wide-open space where housing moguls have birthed their financial dreams, it's essential to have the scoop on the latest trends. For now, two things are taking center stage: short-term rentals and vacation rentals. Remember this buzzword: Airbnb. It's just a taster of the direction rental property investment is heading.

Short-Term Rentals: Not so Short on Returns

Now unless you've been vacationing out in Mars, or feasting your ears exclusively on hard rock music of the 80's, you have most likely heard of Airbnb. It's sort of become synonymous with short-term rentals. Of course, they aren't the only ones in the biz. Other platforms including HomeAway, Booking, and Flipkey are there too. But essentially, what these guys have done is perfect the art of making money from short-term rentals.

To put it in your own familiar spiel, think of subletting your place for days, weeks, or a handful of months, not only to that cousin who insists on sleeping on the couch. Short and sweet. The money trickles in rather like a tiptoe- joy-ride, not calamitous- here-today-gone-tomorrow scary dip, that long-term rentals tend to elicit. Clearly, the shift toward short-term lets is fueled by a philosophy of life in motion. The demand from professionals working job assignments on the go, emotional wanderers unwilling to sign lengthy contracts, digital globetrotters, and the general preference of receiving rental money steadily makes for compelling argument should there ever be one.

Vacation Rentals: The New Gold Rush of Property Investment

Now boss, if my opening aimed at emotional appeal, vacation rentals are a heart-stealer. When we talk about vacation rentals, it isn't exactly something new, but the facets to it and the manner in which it is evolving, does make one ride a wave of investment excitement. It sounds cliché, but fast-forward to 2022, vacation homes and bookings are going through the roof! What's stoking the momentum, you ask? With global movements on the rise again after a shared meltdown, the thirst for the world culture,

experiences, and rediscovered appreciation for life is thrilling.
Humans' thirst for leisure, tinged with a novelty of local experiences, ensures that vacation rentals remain a gold mine. Remember, geographical placement isn't really the crux here, it's seasoned with activities that matter; think vineyard stays, forest cabins, beach bungalows, downtown lofts, to rustic farmhouses. Their aesthetic plus their host's living-about insights lure bigger audiences. More than hotel rooms, they offer additional privacy, personal kitchens, a personal touch, and the ability to accommodate larger groups

Online short-term rental sites make these types of rentals a breeze to execute, playing middleman between the owner and the vacation-goer. Long story put simply, vacation rentals can be a regular cash cow.

Wrap the Idea Around Your Brain Before the Wallet

Nevertheless, seasoned property moguls always seem to advise that you do ample research before pouring in cash. All that glitters can sometimes drain it rather un-noticeably. And pal, gosh, you do want to feel like Donald Trump strutting around with his investments, not his blunders. Setting rental rates suitable to your local economy, the nitty-gritty of handling bookings, conscientiously staying aware of city code requirements for safety, cleanliness and soundproofs, dealing with maintenance costs, occupancy tax nuances, and 101 other technical glitches can sneak up uninvited on daydreaming investors.

Also, remember to download the perspective of vacation-goers and visiting professionals. It can come handy when scouring beyond the glossy pictures in decisions regarding furnishing levels and logistical support!

But hey Bro, it isn't all clouds and rain either. Baits dropped cleverly, a lesson smattered here, a lesson smattered there could certainly arm the newbie investor into a formidable enthusiast.

Indeed profits are there for the taking. Life's simply too shortsighted to let lucrative forecasts, such as short-term and vacation rentals, to pass by without a hearty high-five in the property investment rodeo, eh?

Top Notch Trends in Rental Property Investing

You know, just the other day I stumbled upon this thought - How does technology affect rental property investing? Doesn't baffle your mind to consider how far we've come in the realm of tech? Now picture this - apply this advancement onto something like property management. Wonky? Not quite! While it might seem like tying two completely unrelated topics together, you'd be surprised how snugly they blend.

Property management isn't just collecting rent checks especially in the day and age we live. It entails sourcing tenants, handling leases, overseeing maintenance, and—a million other little things you probably don't even realize. As lucrative as the game can be, owning and operating rental properties come with myriad minute hassles and grand stresses. You know, own property, be your own master sort of idea! But as scruffy it appears, there is a silver lining – Technology! Yes, Technology is helping take the grunt out of daily tasks. Let's dive in!

KPI Anyone?

Okay, let's twist our path a bit. Have you noticed the sheer prevalence of tech start-ups disrupting traditional industries? Think Uber, Airbnb and then you have the unpredictable bitcoin (Okay I'm exaggerating, but it's exciting, isn't it?). So, why should the rental property industry sit in the corner amid this techno-charged carnival?

Luckily, we are privy to its golden impact in the property management sphere. Think Key Performance Indicators or KPIs. Specific fool-proof metrics for property management now allow for cleaner, simpler expansion strategy. It sounds pretty slick eh? From rent collection, property listings, dealing with prospective and current tenants and overall property management_ have gone the electronic way. In sum, smarter decisions based on real-time data. Goodbye old chap suspense moments!

Tech wearing Nova's Cape

'Metiers turn easy when tech's handsy.' Okay, I attempted a tech-coined proverb there, but you get my point, don't you?

Technology is not just perfect to gain visibility into a humongous pool of potential renters, but, wait for it… It's transformative. Move over painfully traditional maintenance and communication tactics and make way for automated management software, digital marketing plans, and online-centric advertising forums. Surely, automation, you already know is making heads turn to smart homes. Cobble it up with property management and you have it elementary, seamless and error-free maintaining a consistent, strong digital presence.

Sharing economy stuff and Gig

Throwing a newer nuance to discuss – have you given a thought when I mentioned 'Airbnb' vaguely before?' Jumping in – you now witness progressive turns to the sharing economy "Flabbergasted, are you "Can you remember a time when you used a ride-sharing service like Uber and traveled with an unfamiliar person?" Brush fibers deep into real estate, the same riders' idea descends into sharing economy allowing the use of underused assets which range from sharing extra room to whole properties. Talk about rental arbitrage

Wait, there's even 'Gig'ography captivating short-term cultures. Technology allows owners to customize lease terms based on prospective tenant requirements spewing phrases like "pop-up retail", "work hubs" or "co-working spaces" as smart flexible office options. Doesn't strike very Pied Piper-ish opportunity if you think over, right?

The Green Scene

If green is in 'Key', make a technology which helps us support environmental change. Look no further, my friend, as advancements empower professionals to take control over a property's energy use namely through

Green and sustainable property investments

Fancy some coffee-talk about some intriguing new trends brewing in the world of rental property investing? You see, recently there's been a significant shift towards 'conscious capitalism.' What on earth is that, you wonder? It's about investing money and resources with deeming significant aspects such as environment, society, and governance, a.k.a, ESG criteria. Sounds pretty impressive, right?

So, here's the scoop. This shift in consciousness isn't just evident in our purchasing habits, but it's molding the world of investing, especially property investing.

Here's the Thing About the Green Revolution in Property Investing

In recent years, there's been a serious surge in popularity towards investments that reflect sustainability and have a minimal environmental impact. There is increasing interest in 'green' housing—properties that are eco-friendly and energy-efficient homes. It's about showcasing care, being responsible, and driving sustainable development. So, in the world of property investing, a green building makes for a noticeably appealing offering for potential renters and a promising investment for homeowners. <u>Sound a little far-out? Believe me, it's already happening!</u>

If Green Is Gold, How Precious Are These Green Investments?

Hold on to your coffee cups, friend, because while investing in sustainable, eco-conscious property might seem like a rather meta thing to do, it's basically become a future-proof strategy for investors— it is where the world is naturally heading in!

In light of climate change, homes with a minimal carbon footprint minimize environmental damage while being economically efficient— two attributes making them highly sought after by renters. Plus, numerous jurisdictions worldwide have started offering substantial return-ons maybe in the form of tax reductions for sustainable usage of property. As such, investing in green rental property has become the significant investment trend of note.

Sustainability Is in High Demand. Wondering how?

For the eco-conscious folks (I'm betting anything you're one of them?), 'Is it green?' has become a go-to question for anything new considered potential purchases— especially rental investments.

Nowadays, renters— particularly budding generations of millennials and Gen-Z population, put a premium on a living situation that respects the environment and fosters sustainability. Clean energy aspects, relating to components such as your energy-efficient appliances, green insulation, and solar power generators, currently attributes which pass as green basics for the rent-considering individuals.

Agreed that the upfront costs paving the way towards making your investment property 'green' can be a tad high, but what matters is looking at it from a long-term financial standpoint. When you have enhanced energy savings all for improving indoor quality, also not forgetting your property's potential overall heightened market value because who doesn't relate to attractive tax rebates? Savvy homeowners are latching on!

Green Zoning and Certification— Is it your time to tune in?

Hold your thermos firm, buddy. As it always happens when trends pick up (which in this case means greener and healthier living, and a marked decrease in degradation of environmental amenities), regulators get happenstance clues and initiate changes that affect the wider culture. It's happening with the rental investment market as well!

Various states and cities have started implementing green building codes in an attempt to make every habitable building eco-friendlier and aligned with sustainability goals. What's more, certain programs and fiscal incentives push for ' greener' buildings. For property investments, it's becoming increasingly important to comply with the green building codes to continue attracting intended renters without interruptions.

And how, you ask, is a property considered green? Well, green certifications like LEED (Leadership in Energy and Environmental Design) help easily distinguish eco-friendly properties, which further aids and boosts ratings that generate rent premiums. LEED certified buildings are shown to consummating less energy and water, while providing a lucrative reduction in operation and maintenance costs. And guess what, potential renters fall head over heels knowing that a LEED-certified building suggests it leaves less of an environmental impact. Surely fetches a more significant roi, doesn't it?

Thinking Environmental Assets Over Liabilities

To sum it all up, being eco-minded in your investment property isn't just about doing something decent for the world. Hey, you're also cashing out socially attractive returns over time, creating an irresistible packaging for potential rent-check scribblers. Science suggests a 'green shift' coming— society is showing escalating focuses on environmental sustainability. Preemptively investing into environmentally sound property, compiling for yourself above-average financial refunds, potentially witnessing increased tenant satisfaction due to a positive living condition — it all fits in nicely. So, how's your appetite for some green-building coffee surfaced all through these incentives for green, invincible actions of sorts? Witness 'sustainability' getting to 'prosperity,' undeniably declaring itself the key realm to property investment!

Proactively engaging in sustainable practices betters case scenarios for property improvements and reductions of inherent property-related risks. All evidence to the score that choices made as such keep 'future-readiness' intact while lending a hand on the driving wheel brought on by wicked innovation and forecasting subsequent business reputations — because retrospectively examining downlines will only be unnecessary taking tashes on rent receipts, right? Supposed to be greener grass magic and bluer-sky dreams!

When it comes down, it's your time on ticking opportunities to amass energy savings and accolade-ready reductions on ghgs! Jump on, take on those biodegradable building reembraces coming off clean on cups and pledging with the eco property spike—from where we're sitting, dwelling on persistent green and inclusions are something world-weary renters desperately request having on—a sustainability stake off space lease creates future-proof rifts!

Chapter 19: International Rental Property Investing

Opportunities and challenges in international markets

I thought we could take a little time to talk about International Rental Property Investing. Yup, you got that right. Now it's no longer just about buying that duplex down the road. This direction can be absolutely thrilling but comes with its own sets of opportunities and challenges. Let's dig in, shall we?

The Global Landscape

Move aside local real estate deals! International real estate investing offers a brand-new set of adventures. With an accommodating legal system, good infrastructure, and stable political situation, numerous countries along with a rising GDP can be potentially inflation-beating investments. Consider places like Panama, Thailand, or even Turkey. These places are going big on dividends. Absolutely thrilling-right?

And let's not forget the unique cultural experiences. The food, the people, the language. All these right at the doorstep of your investment. Picture owning a fancy condo near Thailand's great beaches. Coconut in hand, watching the beautiful sunset. Makes one daydream!

The Pros or Opportunities

Speaking of dreaming, let's be a little rational and review the awesome opportunities which lie ahead.

Diversification is Key

With an international property, you've got assets 'scattered' to reduce risks. Ideally, when the US market tanks, you're hoping other overseas markets (like in Europe) you invested in stay firm. Safety first, right?

Some Economical Benefits

Okay, assume the local real estate market where you got the lease is on an up. Does your dollar stand a chance against the local currency? If "Yes", then, my friend, you're in for juicer deals. Heck, you may even enjoy costs of living cheaper than back at home. Worth pondering over.

Feel that Ex-Factor. Be Exotic!

Own that vacation spot in Greece you've always dreamed of and you're all set! Your own home, for those holiday seasons and maybe friends too. When it's sail-away season, you can always place it out on Airbnb.

The Cons or Challenges- They Await!

Alright. Enough with the nice things. Is International Rental Property Investing challenging?

Absolutely! Let's dive deep, shall we?

Regulations: Framework, Paperwork & Lots of Understanding!

National, regional and local property laws vary dr…

Now speaking about legislation-the not so good part. To purchase a property outside your national boundaries might mean excessive paperwork and legal hassles. Plus, understanding a rental system thousands of miles away, along with knowing safety regulations, insurance requirements…the whole nine yards! Daunting chills incoming? Waiting to say:

"Mother, is that unpleasant man coming around again?"

Lingual Barriers: Is Hola the only Spanish you know?

Well, have that covered. Even if the English language graph looks impressively tall, snags can still appear out of thin fog when discussing property-level stuff with the locals. Worst part? This can invite blunders you might not want to remember.

Scams: Be Aware!

Ever watched those Hollywood flicks where corny overseas businessmen rip off ingenuous investors completely? If you grasp that reality chain, you'd realize unwary investors are the premium 'beef-steak' for local cons. More than often, they manipulate foreign laws to trap unsuspecting landlords, so be wary.

Need More Visitations

Not going to forget, oversee an overseas property involves more travel. Spot inspections can be steeply pricey.

Legal considerations and regulations

Our conversation today will explore some of the legal considerations and regulations to keep an eye out for when you're eyeing a dangle carrot across the border. Heading into international waters can be thrilling but without a closer look, at law and order ruling over these foreign lands, it might feel like navigating a maze. In short, brace yourself and dive right in!

Are you familiar with the phrase, "When in Rome, act as the Romans act"? Let's retrofit, say "When investing abroad, stick to local regulations", sounds familiar, doesn't it? When you invest your greens (or yen, euro, what have you) abroad, giving the local trade laws quite the honour (almost like carpet entry, say) is Order of the day. You know, taxes, rules regarding property rights, local laws around rent control, and even the tiny bits about transferring and converting money from one currency to another.

Now, here's a head-scratcher - tax. Aren't we all too well-acquainted! Well, for starters, every country has a different line about property taxes. While you're scouting the overseas property or even just fantasizing in your lounger, find out about what the local taxes look like. Throw your hat and ask around about local requirements, tax values, and don't pinch pennies in hiring a tax consultant, if you really have to. It can save you quite a setback! Reminder: do not forget to discover all there is about those horrid hidden taxes, friend.

Trademark me these buzzwords - Property Rights and Ownership Laws. Sweated right out of a legal thriller screenplay, these words reckon extensive diligence. No cha-cha-cherry-picking, thorough scrutiny needed. Countries may have diverse laws for native citizens versus foreigners in the arena of property owing permissions. Get hawk-eyes for understanding the ropes of government regulations about you, a foreigner, owning a piece of land or structure (or probably both). Remember that picture I painted about navigating a maze?

Rent control laws and the consequent regulations should be your next stop. After buying real estate overseas doesn't end there, right? The game is managing and probably exploiting that rental property hence the importance of thorough knowledge of local rental markets and individual rent control laws. You wouldn't want a veritable nightmare with rents too masked to even get returns from or even policies hindering you from shooting tenants, huh?

Right! Now about conversion and transfer of money: each nation has its own barn-and-bale set of regulations regarding how money can be transferred in /out or converted between currencies. Navigating these regulations may at the outset look daunting but get into the boots and you'll manage, one step at a time. You can even get a financial consultant to guide you through this. Accents and idioms of international financial sand dunes can get a tad too dense for palates, better safe I say.

Just imagine this: Waking up to a fresh breeze from your beachfront property in Bali. Or, lingering over your morning coffee as you monitor the income stream being generated by your exquisite condo in the heart of Paris. Sounds enchanting right? Well, let's convert that daydream into a carefully executed financial strategy!

Precisely, we're going to dive into 'International Rental Property Investing.' Yep that's right, not only mixing an old-fashioned love for real estate but tossing in a pinch of wanderlust for good measure!

Seriously, all oneiric whispers aside, investing in overseas properties, particularly as rental investments, comes with a thrilling world full of opportunities buoyed by potentially hefty financial returns. But that's not to downplay the serious hurdles that will unquestionably bob up along the journey. Let's navigate this world—the vibrant, the stringy, and the sludgy aspects of international rental property investment, together.

Setting the Stage: Is International Rental Property Investment a Good Strategy?

If you ask Google that question, you will come across two distinct groups of opinions—the supporters who passionately advocate the benefits of diversifying wealth and enjoying lucrative capital gains, and the skeptics who strongly warn against exposing oneself to avoidable risks. It's like a choir that hasn't yet perfected their harmony.

Simply, snap shut Google and return 'home'. What has always been your own personal reason for investing in properties up till now? I assume it's something beyond "owning something cool," correct? I mean believe me, everyone loves a dream house. But remember, you're an investor! Is making a plentiful return on investment ringing any bells?

So, let's first dial down and understand the notable benefits of considering international property in the first place:

Capital Appreciation: A minor escapade around the world will reveal there's a gigantic property appreciation potential resting elsewhere—in countries whose real estate markets are fledgling skyrocketing daily.

Diversification: Tell me, why store all your eggs in one basket? Investing overseas enables you to amass a rich palette bundled from various economies and markets.

Attractive Rental Yields: This is us—we jump up, excited! Rental properties offer a regular stream of passive income.

And the Contortion?

Legal Implications: Each country's property laws vary.

Manageability: Geographic distance sure has its mystique but comes with a nuance of complications, like management and maintenance guilt.

Foreign Exchange Risks: Currency exchange rates stand just as dynamic as your desire to visit every country in the globe.

Building—and Scaling the Success Ladder

Keep an eye, or two—heck, borrow more if need be,—on the potential market booms elsewhere, but ensure you don't stray too far by spending carelessly. Instead, roll your sleeves and get down into mastering simple strategies like navigating the property laws, foreign mortgages and so much more.

Choosing the Right Destination: You must maintain clarity when it comes to region, country, and moreover, neighborhood. Weight up property interest levels, government and economic stability, property prices and any noticeable industry trends.

Legal Complexities and Cultural Nuances: Jumping the legal hoops can be one complex limbo exercise. Hire bilingual professionals to guide you through the local property laws while also tap into investment specialists and local property agents.

Capital and Cash-Flow Management: Aim for markets providing progressive openings for property value appreciation and rental potential—even better if freshly unlocked. Also, arm yourself for dealing with foreign exchanges and readying measure for hedging risks.

A Great Property Management Team: Don't resist hiring a trusty overseas property management team. They'll undoubtedly wrestle essential tasks such as tenant support, network maintenance, managed taxes and keeping your overseas liability at much nil.

Chapter 20: Future of Rental Property Investing

Predicting industry trends and changes

I've picked up some interesting insights into trends and predictions for the industry's future and thought you might want to puzzle over them too.

So, get comfortable and join me on this venture into understanding the enthralling world of rental property investments going forward.

The Green Approach: Sustainable Properties

A topic very green and trendy these days is this idea of ESG investing, a triple bottom line focused on making Environmentally (E), Socially (S) responsible, and good Governance (G) decisions. Rental property hasn't stayed behind in catching some ESG trends in moving towards a more sustainable future.

People today aren't just asking for properties, they're after environmentally friendly homes. Energy-efficient homes, minimal residues, renewable resources, gardens with native plants, water conserving installations, use of organic, recycled, and locally found materials appraises rental values. Beyond occupants' health and comfort, sustainability attracts tenants hiking landlords' return on investments comparatively over conventional offerings. Despite slight advancements costs, its disposition for prospective profitability, the influence on decisions progressively make green rental properties preferred and common-place.

The Rise in Flexible, Short-Term Rentals

We are living through an era when almost everything (economy, work, lifestyle, and travel trends) is flexi n lean. Attributing to the "renting economy," the hype for short-term rentals ain't dusting away anytime soon. Platforms like Stayz and Airbnb offer something the majority-trending millennial generation – or rather all walks of life – is ordering today - variety and experiences over ownership!

Thanks to these platforms, investors often achieve higher rentals on a short-term arrangement compared to a long-term lease, pretty lucrative, eh? And the upsides doesn't stop there, flexibility allows you to use the property personally whenever isn't tenanted.

We're smacked amidst the crossroads, where the community zeal challenges tranquillity. With involved regulation rectifications and balancing execution, the sector may dangle, nonetheless ebbs and flow through enhancement and growth.

Urbanization and Smart Cities

Predictably, the new gen runners more likely to settle and build their future in cities. Consequently, Urban housing, commercial hubs, smart cities and rental over ownership shall soar pursuing self-maintaining rental investments.

For mindful building investors, creating compact-built projects encompassing hi-energy saving, accessibility, affordability, relevant utilities, environmental synchronisation stands up favourable equation with such residential norms' demand.

Urban community intercourses integrated with tech, sustainability, flexibility aspects assure calculative amenability construing long-run profits for yourself in rental property.

Innovations in property management and investment strategies

You know, lately, there has been a monumental surge in interest rates and property investment intrigues. So let's reconnect again by discussing the future of rental property investing; we'll delve into some neat innovations in property management and financial game plans!

We also have sophisticated software programs promoting the efficient collection and calculation of rent – reducing default risk and enhancing financial transparency. And then, some absolutely shrewd apps on your smartphone can aid efficient property management – a whole universe of convenience in your pockets.

Innovative Investment Strategies

Moving on, I thought I'd also chip in the rising innovation trends in investment strategies stocking up the hat. Let's face it; no one wants to miss out on the ride along the hi-fi tech-investment highway.

Here then is another eye-opener; sale-leaseback transactions—a sort of double espresso treat, where you retain use of possession while yielding wealth and liquidity. Yeah, off-loading properties to REITs and leasing them back pretty much formulates the essence of sale-leaseback tactics.

Then, there is the trend of Co-Living Spaces—imaginative, adaptive shared housing models. They present a progressive housing solution style open-generation lofts and feature security, community, and flexibility. This hyper-efficient footprint lies globally at the function of sustainability (and affordability).

Environmental Consciousness Declaring Future Statement

I'd dare say, at the start of this decade, green energy efficiency was pretty much of a penny drop, wasn't it? Well, currently, it's shaping up to be the wealthy north star of property investing. Solar power and eco-smart buildings stand central to this new junction in the property value alley. And I think they might soon pick up irresistible steam.

Turns out, more and more investors seek environmental consciousness and sustainable footprints as critical factors into their figures. Lenders, in return, are pushing in for better sustainable enhancement reports on properties. I'd say, the future secures up here well enough, crossing big greener capital checks!

Technology Meets Tradition

No doubt, real-estate remains, traditionally and virtually, unchanged through significant timelines. Yet, the prospect where innovative technology meets this classic terrain is taking a big charge by the day.

Imagine new-age tech spaces fast colluding with economic robustness within the property walls. Sounds quite e-futuristic right? With steady swings in AI, drones, virtual realities, autonomous cars, the investment ring in rental property seems fertile enough for tech-bucks ready to bloom.

Overall, I just thought cementing up between traditional sticking-points and the state-of-art tech corridors places us grand to usher the shifting dynamics. Because, as we leap into this changing tide-rider, Property investments strategies will not just remain time-haven-options but also negotiate win-win social outturns, too philosophical, eh?

My standpoint, keep evolving, keep innovating, because novel digital merriment platforms demand breaking into refreshing intervals in the way how traditionally we view property investment - mixing-in the right tenants, co-living realities, nurturing intelligent systems, promoting eco-forwardness.

Feel the gravity of changing game already? Sure bet, rental property investing is no longer confined to buy-to-let policy but also positioning wealth into high-efficiency premium.

Hold on tight, because we're about to take a deep dive into an exciting topic - the future of rental property investing and how we have to adapt to evolving market conditions. yes, connecting all those dots which decide your return on investment is rather complex. Don't groan though; buckle up and come with me on this ride along an exciting, potentially fruitful investment path. Without the illusion of pulling a magic rabbit out of the hat, it's fair to declare upfront that this sector - just like any other - requires constant adaptation to an evolving set of market dynamics and conditions. But...picture this - Bending right on roller coasters. Rush of adrenaline, eh? Navigating through the rental property market can be equally thrilling - consider it a financial roller-coaster that upswings on shrewd future savvy intellect and relevant insight.

Rental Property Investing: Past, Present, and Future

Hang on because we will travel through time for this.

Revisiting the past: Traditional Bricks and Mortar

Initially, most rented premises were tied up in commercial units or other bricks and mortar. There's a natural comfort with the concrete structure your doors pushed and knob turned. It was — and to a decent extent, continues to be mostly based on assured returns – derived from industrial, retail units, or residential long-term lease cuts.

Mimicking the present: Decoding the "Live, Work N Play"

Consider this buddy, lifestyle patterns have actively decoded this simple phenomenon playing around: "Live, Work, n Play." Rental scenarios changed with shifting professional demographics significantly. Gen X or Millennial Professionals valued nifty temporary pads near work areas more or coworking spaces instead of long structured bouts. Luxury residential areas over office skyscrapers began reaping yielding returns. A catchy phrase won't harm; many even named it as Co-Living Takes Corona Hit With A Pinch Of Netflix Salt - making urban jungles comfortable whilst inching towards impending lockdowns!

Fastforward to the Year 2030-ish(Extra points for Audrey Irony!)

Breaking-In the Coded Evolution

Predicting a future straight as an arrow is somewhat trickier than anticipating the next season on Game of Thrones. However, considering shifting socio-economic landscape, digital transformations and heaps more predicted evolutionary snags, certain patterns emerge.

Rental property investing - Evolution or revolution?

So, here's the deal – the projected transformations are surging towards an urbanization boost. Alongside this swells the need for affordable housing. However, affordability lies relatively deeply entwined with relative cost-benefit considerations.
Renting can become an attractive alternative to purchasing a property** Imagine, affordable living moves asking for cheaper maintenance, lesser down payments, strategized financial elasticity - an easy formula hinting leasing over ownership, opening up a completely urbanized demography for rental investors to capitalize on.

The climacteric steer will also interflow from shifts in Economic Stratum. The millennial boost impacted significantly too - Ownership patterns are gradually changing per as the world progresses with age, making rental property more flexible & accessible.

Use of Digital-First Attitude!

Its digitized dart everywhere! Hence directly peppering the rental investment phase like no other, buddy. COVID broke across technology shackles making digitization key to almost everyone, right?
Selective target-based online property configurations integrated online platforms have begun to feature where traffic flows are tracked minutely - sort of putting predicted ROI straight in the Investor's Inbox!

A disruptive paradigm of Cryptocurrencies is seen entering the mainstream, affording opportunities to break into hitherto inaccessible markets. Think about it, mate! No Border Limits anymore! Exchange Currency endangers powerful commodity-based tokenized economics to openly invite everyone to invest in profitable blocks away from home cases - Rental investment options just stuffed grocery shelves grocery at the glocal Mart!(coined Global + Local spiced colloquialism)

Future FinTechnology

Approach with care though; turbulence is expected in Initial Currency Recessions unless when Cryptos convert in universally accepted trade moderators(Shhh•• Bitcoin). Professional investors ensure combusting costs incurred remain relatively minimal compared to conventional ways pushing regulatory authorities adopting validated cross-country crypto cross exchanges for rental digitized assets easing access then ever!

To cut the long tech-story short; crucial ways navigating around the see-saw of rental property investment can be easier assuming buddy-to-buddy chit chat rolls professionally highlighting our plain insight reading obvious oncoming micro housing need spurn with taste of future embedded conveniently cheering realities show around the economic-stratum and emerging digital phenomena, by braving interim push-button receivable turmoil meanwhile may true happen returning profit levels pragmatically. ``Keepin' watch, eye on tomorrow adapting rental property investment techniques shaping assertive financial health status thereon`` owes less to a jittery emotional ticker ticking running beside then the intellect, foresee the future as realistically possible.

A Transforming Field

Rental property investment delivers a hefty punch for investors detecting letting things fall in place naturally, tuning rather auto tuned trendset path. It's exciting, vast, demanding but delivers real long term sustainable investment punches.

Chapter 21: Balancing Rental Property Investments with Other Ventures

Diversifying investment portfolios

Man, do I see a smashing smile on that face! You probably just bought a new rental property, right? Impressive! You're off to a strong investment start there but you definitely need to pick that brain to remember a crucial rule of investing. What rule you ask?

Let's summarize it in one distinct word: diversification!

"Don't put all your eggs in one basket"; you've certainly heard this term, right? Well, it's beyond the mundane common saying. In investment circles, it carries an enormous amount of weight. It talks about the sweet science of diversification. Now the real deal here is how you would balance your rental property investment with other lucrative ventures. Let's take a calming breathe together (Yes! Breathe in Breathe out) and chew profoundly on this mind-bracing topic.

"Rental Property Can't Feed - If He's the Only Thing That Leads."

Oh boy! Rental properties are a slam dunk! Aren't they fantastic with their steady cash flow? You absolutely right! But there's a downside that maybe you've not thoroughly considered. I guess you are eager to know that, ha, sure thing buddy – there's a catch and this is important to grasp(!)

See, as fantastic as this venture might seem, it leaves you vulnerable to surprising and somewhat perturbing risks e.g., bad tenants (ain't none got no time to babysit such 'beauty' right? Wink!), to name just one. So constantly keeping all your bucks in the rental property drawer isn't cute buddy. We need to spice up the financial cooking and add some flavorsome pours to the investment game.

Let's break and dig into diversifying your investment portfolio.

Playing a Shrewd Game in the Financial Field

Rule of thumb for a real sophisticated investor: don't be vulnerable to hidden risks or mark yourself an easy target. How? By distributing your assets across multiple various investments. Maybe bonds, retirement accounts, foreign investments…you name it. Believe me when I say this, my dear friend— playing a shrewd game in the financial field is playing it safe. It's shielding your eggs—oops, I mean investments! — from those unknown disaster situations we dread to think about. Imagine a scenario where you lose all investments due to over-reliance on one type.

Pretty gory, right? Ha! We don't want that, as we said before – positive breath in!

Introducing various types of investments decreases your financial vulnerabilities helps you exponentially at multiplying those satisfying green notes— dolla dolla bills y'all.

Roundtrip to Growth: An Intertwining Journey

Hold up! One second before you fly into the plane burning with over-diversification hot flames.

In anticipation of diluting those risky operations, it could get ugly; okay, maybe uglier. Getting too excited with diversification has the potential to rippled your great growth adventure and we not about signing up for a disaster buddy!

"I need to inquire; is there a risk of the value being diluted or the profits declining drastically?" That is the blazing question"- a quote to mull over, right? Finding balance for an optimal financial behavior is the true gem to cheer on here. Walk through the knives edge of spreading enough dough around without spewing it in excessiveness where it hinders you from reaching the rich, fulfilling final anthem—wealth growth.

Diversifying Perspectively

Alright Yoda, let me wrap up our conversation of potential financial scrolls tenet from disturbance apart.

Renting wisely— Own it, manage when it touches responsibility, Accordion investments for optimized gain…Hold up! Accordion investments? Thumbs up, fellow finance pupil!

By following phased investing strategies, you allow gradual enhance in purchasing land premises and progressively reduce the balancing gamble. Not loading all financial heavies into one is a scripturally smart approach. Pull out some portion and slide it towards high-profit yielding commodities like currencies.

Did stocks even cross your mind! Nice! You sexy and you know it(!). The gamble in foreign countries relating in buying stocks with possible colossal return of investments aids in healing wounds that might have been inflicted in your stay of having rental properties by some imaginary asteroids.

Buy government and corporate bonds, cut it well and slump a heavy weighting to commence a vacation interest while a cold sip in retirement enjoyable pleasures.

Balancing risks and rewards

I hear that you're thinking about pouring some money into rental property investments? That's a great way to see significant gains, but with any investment, there comes a level of risk. Let's chat on how to balance out your rental property pursuits with your other ventures so you're not placing all of your eggs in one basket.

First and foremost, it's essential to have a well-rounded investment portfolio filled with various types of investments. You're no newbie to this game, you know that diversification is key. You don't want to tie your financial future too much on one particular venture — even if it's a promising property down the road.

The Pros of Rental properties

Let's talk advantages first. Unlike some of your hectic investment ventures (Yeah, I'm looking at you, crypto market!), rental property investments could provide an ongoing income flow. They can also deliver inciting tax advantages and boast potential for appreciation. Not to mention, you even could pay off the property while your tenants gradually fund your mortgages for you. Sounds sexy, right?

Well, as tempting as it may be to dive right in and pour your money into multiple rental properties, it's essential to have balanced investments. After all, we don't want a bleak-looking stock portfolio, do we?

Just like in love, variety is the spice of investment life

Think of getting various investments just like ordering a much-celebrated multi-flavors ice cream sundae. There's the much-loved classic vanilla - these are your safe bet investments, such as bonds and a mix of low-risk stocks. Topped with spicy hot fudge - these are riskier but more profitable prospects, such as certain stocks or new ventures.

I know rental properties are fascinating, probably that everyone is blabbering about. It might be like exotic lavender honey instead. Intriguing right! But before you go for three or four scoops of that, ensure you have the classic staples to balance. It acts as a safety net if suddenly the sweet allure to rental properties sours.

The Complicacy Associated with Rental Properties

Besides the fact that rental property investments tie yourself heavily to a single type of "vanilla" (Looking at you real estate sector), they also possess unique risks compared to other ventures.

I mean, it's a 'people burden' at best. You'll eventually have to deal with various rental-specific issues – late or unpaid rent, property damage, legal intricacies, and difficult tenants. Once the investment deal is signed, you can't just move out of it as quickly as selling shares when the going gets rough.

Remember, it's like signing up for a roller-coaster ride, those bumps, and unexpected free jumps are part of it.

The Attraction of the Rental Planet!

Looking on the brighter side here, some of these issues might be minimized by hiring a property manager or securing skilled legal counsel. They get things under control by dealing with vacancies, tenants, and property issues. Sure, they come at an extra cost, stripping your profits, but added peace of mind may very well be worth it.

Oh, great point! Rental properties are beneficial in providing predictable revenue streams and tangibility! If you deal smartly with the complicated hiccup balls thrown by it, the returns can be pretty significant. Remember the key: Proceed with caution!

Bringing Balance to the (Investment) Force

Conversational ramblings aside, if you're going to pick up rental properties, be sure they're only one part of a varied investment game-plan. Keep broadening your ranges of real estate ambition beyond residential properties to featuring commercial exploits. Act smarter by including bonds, shares, commodities, ETFs, or money market funds.

Now put all these ensembles cast into your neat profile vibe; ensures you have solid protection even when one sector goes haywire.

Well, it's high time to invest but in balance—You know the drill! Prepare in advance, arm yourself against risks, maintain the right balances, look at the blueprint right and boom! You're all set to sit back for sipping on the sweet success milkshake concocted from diversified materials. Here's wishing buckets-full of success for your ventures!

Property investments have the potential to earn a capital appreciation and a consistent flow of income if managed properly. But here's the trick - finding the perfect balance between these and other business endeavors.

Now, when we're talking about incorporating rental properties into functions like your wealth-building strategy, it's a concept as delicious as a double-cheese pizza on a Friday night! However, I'll shoot straight, it's not all warm and fuzzy. So, let's chat about how you can avoid becoming overwhelmed and how you can maintain just the perfect harmony among your rental property investments and your other ventures.

Get Your Financial Foundation Rock Solid First

Hey, you wouldn't build a house on sand, would you? Exactly! Before we even aim at diversifying your investment streams, you must work on setting the financial infrastructure needed for diversification. Get a super check on that emergency fund, pay off debts and yes, keep enough to meet your daily expenses.

Only once we have ticked across these, you bring in the calculation for disposable or free cash. This is what we can consider while calculating real estate investments.

Let's Crunch Those Numbers, Shall We?

I'm sure you don't want to have your wealth tied up solely in hard assets like brick and mortar, right? So, before you plunge into buying that rental property, it's crucial to do a little number dance. You need a prudent investment and financing strategy so as not to be excessively leveraged, keeping nice liquidity and capital reserves aside for pitfalls and opportunities alike.

Remember folks, real estate is a long-term venture, so do keep any notes about early-stage market conditions (especially) the rental comps and occupancy rates in the local market right beside your pillow!

Diversification, Your Safety Net

So, what's your investment game plan? A cluster of stocks, shares or some classic entrepreneurial investments already worked up? Well, letting these avenues diversify, while your bread and butter remains unaffected is just the pleasure of beholding your wealth multiply by the day!

Remember, the key here is not to put all your country chickens in one basket, eh? Grab a risk mitigating investment class (like the bonds) but don't forget to let your money run a fabulous gamble on those beautifully wide venture horizons (like startups).

Physical Property Investments and Farthing Rewards Positively
Oh! Who's been able to resist the charm of positive cash flow, huh? Trust me, as magic runs in the leafy town of Hogwarts, so does a positive cash flow make your house income-generating! Long term mortgage vs monthly rental like payments; they just steer clear to bulk profits gradually, padding up your venture basket much evidently.

But be warned, being a landlord is a hat you must don with care, incurring not just profits but property tax, association dues, maintenance costs and periodic vacancies as well.

Expert Edges Can't Hurt, Right?

Some days nothing beats a good scroll, I'm right? Putting few marketing dollars in building relationships and networks are every bit those pennies' worth of wisdom. After all, your business network is much more rewarding and experienced. They could fluently guide you through the intricate soup of acquiring the property with the best rate of return.

In the process, they could also guide you through transforming these higher costs into opportunity zones and tax advantage plans, neat isn't it?

Remember: Balance Is Harmony

Hands on heart; competing ventures, investments or engaging jobs are equally essential, so don't wrestle with the dread of time or energy management. Here's my secret recipe which aced my investment portfolio and I'm happily sharing it with you.

Think of it like this, how about buying an occupied turn-key rental, guaranteed by the seller? Tad time off to manage the unit yourself! Or employing an enviable property manager, those friendly loans from your local bank. Just perfect to accumulate the reserves, isn't it? And while they do their jobs, you glide as nothing but a virtual landlord. Sweet, ain't it?

Property investment can be a winsome addition bringing more beautiful feathers on your wealth cap. However, like everything else in life, it's important to maintain perspective and a healthy balance. Because we all know, only in balance do we weave the best tales of success, right?

Chapter 22: Creating Passive Income and Financial Freedom

Identifying passive income opportunities in rental properties

Have you ever really thought about what 'financial freedom' means? I mean, it's a phrase we hear thrown around like confetti at a wedding, but when you get into it, what's its essence? Underneath all the frilly 'lifestyle' magazine vocabulary, financial freedom is essentially about making your money work for you, instead of you working for your money. Is there anyone who wouldn't want that?

There is no one-size-fits-all solution here, but one fantastic avenue to consider is generating money from rental properties for passive income.

What do we mean by 'Passive Income'?

Imagine you're the manager of a band. You don't sing, you don't dance, you're not out there with a guitar — but essential in creating a successful product (in this case, the band's moment in the spotlight). People love the music and buy it in droves. The cash flow continues to roll in even when you—or your band— are sleeping. That is passive income.

Miracles by Mistake: The passive investment

Whether we're talking online businesses or stock investments, quite often, the main foundation of creating an 'egg nest' lies in understanding passive income. Passive income is making money while chillin' on your couch half the globe away—are you catching the financial fishing line here?

Rental properties naturally tick all these boxes. Say, for example, you purchase a house or an apartment. You're not necessarily living there – but when you rent it out, it starts to generate income: Someone else (the tenant) pays you rent, which covers your mortgage, taxes, and maintenance expenses.

Cooking with gas, hah? That's how you have your financial cake and eat it too.

Identifying Passive Income Opportunities in Rental Properties

Well, the key phrase here really should be calculating returns. Dummies, or logic? Well, both acts quite harmoniously here if done right. So, if you're willing to take a Mathletics crash course, jump onboard. A whopping 1% return on your investment monthly is your sweetspot. You'll ask: how do I get that? Well, research, diligence, and a fair deal of legwork are often needed.

Let's try breaking it down, shall we:

Let's say you purchase a property for $200,000 and want a $2,000 return on your investment every month (which is 12% yearly, by the way.)

First, this requires smart buying—identifying undervalued assets which are valued lesser than their possible opportunities, doing your research and estimations.

Next, use realistic cash flow modelling. You don't want your pockets dried out taking care of a sick property, do you? You'd need to take into account all predictable expenses (utilities if covered, taxes, homeowners association fees, vacancies, repairs, property management, etc.). A left-field guideline says to chuck at least 50% of a unit's rental income on these expenses—no rainbows over missing undertakings over calculus, yes?

Try multi-unit investing:

The act of pursuing a single tenant can drain your energy and enthusiasm. If you've got one rental and that tenant disappears in the middle of the night, that's a 100% vacancy rate—you're effed. But a multi-tenant complex- that's dope. Someone's got to pay. Swig surprise? Purpose-built multi-unit properties often offer far greater returns than the same outlay invested in single-unit prospects.

Locations and Evictions:

Location is a far heavy contributor to your property's ultimate rental income- plain vanilla, eh? Good neighborhood homes always get good vibes on paper—a popular school district, low crime rate, convenient proximity to community elements such as parks, playgrounds, restaurants, cafes, and shops, will drill up rentals like water in a desert.

Also, have a process for quickly ejecting a bad/ troublesome/ late-paying renter and replacing them with an all-good tenant rapidly. Compare eviction laws across nations, too! In some regions, the pulse quickens a bit sluggish—not the quickest of trees.

One more tiny winy bit—make entertainment an Integral of your properties' planning principle. Smart automation, controlled thermostats, water purifiers, not-so-crazy home security applications, great doorbells all make the home, yea? Stick note to remember that renters aren't looking for just any old cave!

I've got some good news!!! You can actually create an additional stream of income, I'm talking about Passive Income. How cool would it be flushing money into your account while you sleep, spend time with your family, or go on a dream vacation? Great, right! One of the most effective ways to create this kind of income is through real estate investing. I'm sure you've heard the millionaires' secret - Almost 90% of all successful investors made a buck or two through real estate and now it's your time.

The Core Power of Real Estate Investment!

Here's something you should always keep in your mind; the greatest asset of real estate investment is leverage. Unlike many other investment vehicles, with real estate, it's not you who's making the full payment; it's mostly funded using borrowed capital i.e., leverage. Thi allows you to buy bigger properties, for modest amounts, yielding wealth explosions down the line! I mean, where else can $20,000 bring you ownership of a $100,000 property?! Answer is nowhere!

So, Let's Break Down How Real Estate Investing can create Passive Income?

Sure, understanding these techniques will position you on the path of financial independence. We explore a few here:

Rental Real Estate Investing

This style is as old as land ownership itself; a property is bought and then rented to a tenant. You, being the owner or the landlord, will receive a monthly sum from the tenant. Just one necessary thing - there's a level of management that comes along, but hey, with renting apps and property managers, it isn't as daunting as it might sound.

Real Estate Investment Trusts (REITs)

Imagine them as mutual funds for real estate. They're mostly traded on the public stock exchange. So, everyone has access. Here, you own portions of a estate building portfolio. Given their liquidity (selling stocks with a click), it's ideal for those who want in on real investing arena but detest the management part.

Real Estate crowd funding

You want a piece of the real estate action, but can't afford a property? Congrats! Crowdfunding platforms enable you to contribute together with other investors. Sure, in a way, it's similar to REITs. The distinction is that with crowdfunding, it's all about particularly chosen developments vs. general portfolios.

171

Making the Investment Call

Of course, First step first - be sure you have the wits, research, and demeanor for this field. Are you good with logistics or okay dealing and negotiating terms?

Start by dipping your toes on REITs or maybe even consider some other tried-and-true investments like bonds or low index mutual funds. No harm or shame to being extra careful.

Then figure out your investment "game plan." Are you leaning towards single-family homes, townhouses, commercial buildings or apartment complexes? Every single choice carries its sets of pluses and minuses. So sure, be prepared.

Know your market!!!!The figures will show you everything. Let data such as rental yields, price history, local economics, employment rates all induce clarity to your potential locations.

Creating a Steady Cash Flow

It may seem impossible right now, but hundreds of people have attained financial independence via real estate investing. It's about being strategic. So, create a goal.

Start with baby steps, buy a rental property, perhaps? Move towards ensuring the rental income slightly overruns what's necessary for insurance, mortgages and upkeep. That way, you've consistently passive income -

The Breathing Space Found Right There!

With time, bank profits to invest in second properties and diligently reciprocate. Soon enough, you will be positioned uniquely rushing towards financial independence.

Key considerations

Do sweat the small stuff. Brick by brick. Perform extensive due sensitivity, consult an attorney and create contingencies.

Increasing your portfolio holistically and slightly eliminates the odds of going into debt.

Mind the market timing. You do not wish to procure during peaks when possible ROI will be low.

Grasping the Tax Implications

Oh yes, there's no escape from this fella! You'll have to pay taxes; the good news is that real estate caters for enticing tax benefits.

Pay heed to just a crucial variety:

Doors open for Deductions and Depreciations.

Explore Long-term Capital Gains Lower Tax Rates.

Make use of the Rollover: Especially appealing if you maintain real estate long-term.

Let's unravel how you could score this deal, with real estate acting as your wingman.

To step into the world of real estate without fear, it's important to have a good atlas of strategies; cause well mapped is well done!

So, let me share with you 5 top strategies legit successful real estate moguls have been employing for years to build sustainable passive income streams.

Rental Properties

You might have heard this song before since long-term residential rentals remain the main queen on the chess board when we talk about passive income. Simple to understand and lucrative in the long run, this method involves purchasing property and letting it out as residential quarters for a steady influx of rent payments.

What makes this all the more seductive, is leverage - you don't need to bear the burden of full payment, just a percent can be out of pocket. Meaning, as your tenant coughs up their rent each month, they're actually helping you to pay off your loan. Neat, huh?

Rent a Unit, or Room

Want to dip your toes a little less deeply in the waters but still yearn for rental income? Consider investing in a duplex or triplex, live in one part, put on your 'friendly neighborhood landlord' hat and rent out the rest. This strategy – house hacking, in urban lingo – could just give you a positive cash flow.

Sat with a larger home than needs be and a taste for this rental income they speak about? Renting out spaces in your own home you barely use, be it via Annually-Leased Rooms, Airbnb, or another platform, could give you monthly pay cheques, too.

Real Estate Investment Trusts (REITs)

A skeptical beginner you may be, peeking out from your binoculars but treading nimbly around these harder stones of earning big-bang money. This is where REITs give you their card. They're like mutual funds for real estate and perfect to find a smaller, safer pasture to begin with.

Go it alone or pool in with others, and get space in the high turf – shopping malls, offices, hotels! A nice way to dip your toes without having to grit your teeth, eh?

Flipping Houses

This is akin to a daytime drama with an interesting estate interest twist. Ready yourself for the thrill as you buy units at cut-throat low prices, glam them up, then sell them for cash. Tell me you haven't had charm-enough of those fascinating 'House-makeover dramas', look again. There's big money hiding behind the new paint job and patio décor.

This revamp-and-sell strategy requires an eagle-eye for underrated property gems that you can refurbish fruitfully, and above that, haggling, and negotiation skills worth their weight in real-estate gold. But hey, doesn't a precise shot of bonus money sound appealing?

Crowdfunding

Crowdfunding has unveiled a new dawn and proven to be an exciting, innovative option to finance anything from rock bands to tech startups and now, well, properties! Here you benefit from experienced guys doing the hassle of selecting, purchasing, renovating, and managing the property, and give slice-of-pizza dividends. No infamous landlord pressures, but well-drawing income on the drawing board!

Those are your strategies, my would-be real estate gladiator, any of which have the power to earn you a regular pocket filled with passive cash. Remember, Rome wasn't built in a day and nor were mansions built without a hammer; you'll require perseverance and deep diligence, patience, and some nifty crunching of numbers to seduce luck in this field.

And of course, every field head dive includes some head scratches – contract scare-words, legal browsing, dealership quests – but remember, there's no free horse, eh?

This real estate approach is filled with powerful opportunities and whilst demanding fair attention, they're also certainly generous reward givers; whether you take strides or baby steps, the real estate playa has a spot for everyone.

So, are you ready to start 'revelating' on your soon-to-follow concrete journey into real estate passive income? Fasten yourself in, breathe, study, and consider your options. Before you know it, you'll be steady reaping paychecks lounging sipping your fave Oolong tea watching sitcoms. After all, who knew rents could be filled with such thrill, yes?

Chapter 23: Real Estate Investing for Retirement Planning

Incorporating rental properties into retirement plans

I just thought we could talk about something that might pique your interest - planning for retirement. Yes, that sounds a bit too early, right? But believe me, it's never too early to start planning for your retirement. The earlier you start, the more secure your future will be! Now, seeing your curious look, you're probably wondering what all this has to do with real estate. Well, a lot! Real estate investments have become a highly popular strategy for retirement. And your turn has passionately come my friend – considering the incorporation of rental properties into retirement plans.

Why Real Estate?

Now, there are so many ways you can invest for your retirement. There's a guy who advocates investing everything into stocks, another individual that is a diehard fan of mutual funds, while there's me who recommends the woefully underappreciated retirement goldmine— Real Estate!

I know, I know – Real Estate can seem really tricky and a bit intimidating. But listen here buddy, there's a reason why it's often classified as a 'safe' investment. The value usually appreciates over time and provides a cash flow—rental income. How tantalizing does a monthly, steady income sound during retirement? Absolutely faultless, right?

Understanding Rental Property Investments Versus Conventional Retirement Plans

Although fairly low-risk, retirement plans are plagued with limitation and restriction shackles, where real estate enjoys maximum freedom. I understand your pension, 401k, and IRA have seemed more reliable, up till now…

However, buddy, investing in rental property might be your holy financial grail surpassing these!

Rental Properties Perks

Firstly, controlling your investment disbursements isn't an option extended by traditional retirement plans. Set your rents by real estate market trends. Your income can increase with market progression.

Secondly, chalk those storage boxes labelled "Inflation Worries" away for good! The price inflation might chip away the buying power of your retirement savings, but with rental properties, you achieve an excellent hedge against it. In layman's terms, rents usually increase with inflation over the years.

Lastly, do you fancy cash seeming an unattainable archaeological antique from time to time? This means you entirely resonate with illiquid investments then. On the bright side, real estate boasts enticing liquidity and tangibility due to its excellent transaction flexibility compared to assets within retirement accounts guarded by withdrawal penalties.

Imagine— literally building a concrete retirement castle of assets! Glass elevators or patios overlooking Sunrise Blvd you've always dreamed about translating into fruition!!! Bottomline, your strengths should directly impact the retirement well-off-soon-to-be-you!

Challenges Pegged Along

But, uh-oh! It's not all rosy. Involvement comes with its share of pitfalls. Real estate investments and rental properties require getting your hands dirty. Figuratively, buddy! Managing tenants, maintenance headaches along with those tax troubles, and financing conundrums can leave one bewildered, earning disrepute as "time-consuming". These trials often jar people away to distance any investments despite its promising benefits.

Don't be so quick to dismiss it though! Luckily for you and me, real estate investment trusts (REITs) come to the rescue! These are companies that own multiple properties. By investing with them, you can own a piece of the pie without stomaching all the realty sourness.

Tax advantages and strategies for maximizing retirement savings

Remember, your life 2.0 needs just as much lifestyle funding, and possibly more! Real estate investment can be the game-changer you're looking for. Think continuous rent bucks rolling in, or a big fat sell-out jackpot hugging your bank account. Plus, the tremendous tax advantages make it a no-brainer! Let me spill the beans.

Hobnobbing with Real Estate in your Retirement Planning

Did you see the property prices soaring up recently? Ten years from now, they'll be out of sight! Essentially, investing early in real estate pays off big time when you ramp up your retirement strategies. Your salaried days can fund your investment, and post-retirement days can sit back and observe the hefty return fireworks. But, it does help to confess, we can all use some God-forsaken help dealing with hefty investment decisions.

Eye on Some Key Strategies
A Loaded 'ROIsette':

Expenses dent ROI. But if your property gives you regular rental diaries that dance over regular outflow, go for it! Maintenance, insurance... yes yes, they'll pinch your ROI (return on investment). Still, with a steady rental cap, cash flow turns positive and happy, leading your way to Pros shouldering off Vice Consuela.

Depreciation Wonder:

Your on-paper property value dips over time since Uncle Sam believes everything falls apart. While this decline has very minimal real-world implications, it holds onto a bunch of tax benefits. A natural decrease = you, the expert real estate investor, bagging tax write-offs.

Leverage, where stress pours out watercolours:

Leveraging is the rainbow flagged champion - where you buy your property with stellar dreams but minimal cash. Indebted money or some love from modest mortgage rates. No lump sum piles, a cyclic flow will do. Over time, equity seagull falls, untangling financial stress-knots.

Dancing with the IRS: Tax Advantages Coming in Hot and Steamy

A good long dance with the IRS can never mean bad news, eh? Let's break into candor-speaking. TAX BENEFITS! Real estate genuinely welcomes a number of 'em. You wouldn't say no magic-saving wands improving the overall warmth of your retirement snuggle either, right?

Minimize Uncle Sam visitations with diversified retirement investment paths. Intensifying returns wooing your wallets. And, Real Estate Investment? Hats off captain, cool!

Mortgage Deductions:

A luxurious cherry on top! The property Gods fondles optimism raining bounties, letting Uncle Sam pay for mortgages, from land improvements to appreciations. Play your cards, unlock deductions from closing costs and more. Mortgage interest you pay on an investment property is a tax-smart bonus. Enjoy deductions on naughty mortgage expenses grinning your way.

Bustling Depreciation:

Magic of depreciation, mentioned already, is your tax ticket slipping over years of wearing. Bruffy mould stain leaves,

forgetting pricy lingering and simultaneous
tax deductions move-in.

The 1031 Buzz:

Think about trading properties with tax-free laughing upon your
deeds. Sell one, step-in buying another and avoid piling capital
gain vipers via a 1031 exchange.

Is this savvy investment talk stroking desire for sparkling plush
retire? Let's get serious (well, kind of)

Flashing a novice-rake retirement ticket screams preparation
mantras. Be prepared for bidding dear bossies goodbye, and
settling bloomed retirement wonders. Can we bubble some
strategic shooting, retirement knocking much sooner?

Move. First move. Improve. Rinse. Repeat!

Real estate investment roots secure big-time returns catered right
upon retirement gardens. Trust your investment - lodge tax
advantages and luring prizes - a good bet, working miracles for
you while you sleep. So keep up your good vibes dear future
retirees, stay determined to invest stick-ax wonders, and let's
prepare for a gleaming future gateway!

Long-term wealth preservation through real estate investing

You see, apart from the usual retirement schemes we have, there's
something unique that you may find fascinating: Real Estate
investing! It's a fabulous vehicle for conserving long-term wealth,
especially for retirement. Just hear me out!

Why Look at Real Estate Investing?

Okay, I'll not dawdle around and make it really apparent. Real
Estate is tangible! It isn't something digital or paper that you need
to believe it holds a certain value. Buildings, lands, those are real!
Also, the value they hold isn't entirely speculative. Worst-case
scenario, you can live in the property or make use of the land.
Besides, with our ever-increasing population, an investment asset
that's dwindling (they aren't making more land, pal!) is more
prone to appreciate than not.

Another cool thing about this is producing an active
income — renting or leasing out, alongside your principal asset
valuation surges up. Now, who wouldn't like an assured side
income, huh?

178

Plan Venture Carefully

Alright, before you strike all bewildered, understand that real estate investments might seem steep or intimidating if plunged right in. Having a strategic and well-planned approach makes your property investment portfolio favorable and entirely a nice experience.

You know how they say, "It's not the timing of investment but the time in investment that counts." Aim for a long-term horizon. Mark Twain rightly emphasized the ever-increasing land value. Anchoring your portfolio with real estate, you not just invest but own a wealth that you can literally touch, feel, and see whenever you want. Give a leap, pal!

Find Your 'Spot-on'

There is a multitude of approaches that'll adore your chronological stage. At a younger age, speculating lower-priced properties that'll appreciate over time, flips, and rentals are great investment strategies. A middle-aged investor tends to favor growth-oriented commercial properties and REITs (Real Estate Investment Trust). A near-to-retirement player would dwell around income-focused developed properties, rentals and turn enjoys passive income that averts principal depletion. Adjust your strategies according to your risk-taking ability at a certain age. Isn't it all seeming a hinge easier with right planning and strategies?

Trust in Power of Diversity

What say! Having a fallback is one major positive. Complying a part of your overall financial portfolio to real estate is a graceful measure of diversification. It serves as an excellent barrier in an owner's equity.
Just remember here, I am not advocating %100 dipping into properties, instead, striking the right balance would benefit you. Seek various domains—commercial, rental-residential, or REITs—each spotting their unique benefit. Cash flow, appreciation, robust ROI are just a few to name.

Cost & Rectification Matters

Property prices always seem abundant no doubt! But look downstair core matters. Need consistency in payment and vigilant to bear unforeseeable affair properties might throw at us. Litigation, title objections, zoning compliance are inevitable bottlenecks, but don't let that deter you! You got me, right? "Ninety percent of all millionaires become so through owning real estate." - Andrew Carnegie

Look for Skilled Pros

Be it financial planners or seasoned real-estate agents! Outlays rewarded with comfort and smooth investment process hold a capable long-run relativity. Don't forget, not having proper homework is hitch-error having pricey loss chunks. Had any TV episodes saying 'real-home nightmares'? A pro-expert resolves much these at bay and assists in dealing sage like! Professional guide eases retirement planning not as handful or tips-sensitive investing rundown.

Chapter 24: Overcoming Challenges and Staying Motivated

Dealing with setbacks and obstacles

You've dived into the fascinating world of rental property business huh?

I must say, pretty bold buckle you've got under your belt! But, just as with every type of business in this life, we've got mind-boggling challenges to pull through! It almost seems like success comes hand in hand with setbacks… almost like bread and butter. Makes me wonder if 'J.K. Rolling' would've added her inspiring success tale to us without experiencing twelve rejections - yeah you heard it right, twelve blooming rejections.

Now, imagine a box packed up with bulky bricks you've got to carry around while seeking renters for your property, dealing with stubborn or late-paying tenants, handling maintenance and repairs, and conducting routine property inspections. Plus, let's not forget about the legalese, local laws, ordinances, lining up insurance, accounting…the never-ending list goes on. Alright, I'll stop there, don't want to completely drown out your flame for rental properties!

You gotta have the tenacity of a tortoise tightly bound to motivation, always ready to pick it up any second when it falls slip; even carry it on your back like a baby 'cos trust me newbie landlords need motivation as they drink water. (1)

Well then buddy, strap yourself in, remind yourself "Why you started" and let's catapult over obstacles breaking down those bulky bricks.

One Brick Doesn't Tilt the Wall - Dealing with setbacks

First thing straight, never define yourself by your failure, always by your resilience to get back up stronger than ever (2). Here's a truth we've got to taste – every setback is well planted only to create a platform for a comeback.

Why are you letting yourself get locked inside the "I can't" room tapping setbacks where rather your focus should be on hanging around the "I can make it" hallway, setting up proper plans of improvements from setbacks faced?

Investing time analyzing setbacks occupies an invaluable square in running and building successful rental property streaks. It is important to note, you might fail today, succumb to pressure but never fool the error of throwing in all these as flaws instead of phased experiences you've learned (3). Because I tell ya, the fiercer the storm, the taller the palm tree grows.

I am but at arm's length away, stitching you next, the bunch of beads called "never letting setbacks dim the brightness of motivation".

Motivated... keep the ball rolling!

I guess now that you've tasted the bitter herbs of "setbacks meet success", let us drizzle a little honey on that oncoming step - Motivation Era. If success is the destination, motivation is the rocket launcher. And lucky for you it can be obtained from anywhere.

- **Personal Sanity and Construction**

Working as your own boss somehow carries a satisfying plum of rosy motivation skyrocketing your zing across hazy weather striking a surge amongst turbulent challenges (4). Safety resides, self-esteem and small steps eventually turns into mountain ascents.

- **Freedom of Fin's and Flexibility**

Mate, the zeal of economic freedom you catch spreads as a pandemic virus of motivation pushing every breath, every limit hands out (5). Let's not even dig into the lighthearted sensation carried in being carried away with your aspiration of molding your professional pathway after snowballing wealth.

Hey bud, but yeah don't turn all squirrelly. 'Cos 'ere comes the bitter pill no landlord wishes swallowing 'You ARE going to Have Bad Times too'. Perfect trips across a smooth sailing ship of certainty are mere wads of expectations we float.

A way to flood your vibe engulfing consistency demand, you fix eyes-on-your-goal gleaming out challenges faced. Through the heap of bricks covered with challenges when your choice still rests "I am gonna ace this deed" (6) pat your shoulder man 'cos trusts me you're one hell of a spirited lad.

Come on, buzz off that furrowed brow settling creases upon streaks of worry shooting the "give up!" words left lingering. Rent has been, always will be, soaring high and low and it's just another brick off the sack you've got to haul.

There isn't a formula to box success revealing out like lady Pandora curates. Nah mate! Nearly drowning hands in fiddle rolling through trials erected, that's when you begin draining hurdles. Now get up, dust up and climb the ladders, pave cement upon the gold bricks until its neck heightened closer to the pinnacles of success.

I can't resist offering a "show of hands" to anybody investing in the real estate game, particularly the rental property business. It's no secret growing a career in this field offers opportunities for great returns, but it isn't all just without a decent dash of sweat and tenacity. The financial and market challenges that come your way can make you shrug sometimes. But with every worthy goal, there will always be hurdles. The good news is, you're capable of triumphing over these obstacles with effective strategies.

So, buckle up as we cruise through illuminating some of these reliable strategies for overcoming challenges and keeping your motivation in the dynamic world of rental properties.

1. Budget Rigorously and Frequently

Just like going for a weekly health walk, frequent budgeting is a pivotal habit to adopt. See, the rental property market is just similar, where your gains and hiccups make one cohesive whole track that demands attention.

As my grandpa would say: embrace frequent budgeting because it`s like going on a health walk, ensuring your finances are healthy. Swing the ball of budgeting and keep up tab visually with your rental property income and outflow. Time will speak for itself when your landlord-tenanted rental success begins to sparkle.

Keep a constant check on your expenditures. Wait, I know it sounds too much like a boring accountant's job. But there's no possible success if budgets go haywire. From improvements, maintenance, taxes to insurance, retaining an accurate budget book will give you jaw-dropping insights.

2. Intelligently analyze the market scenario and trends

Whether a rooster crows or not, the new day will dawn. Likewise, fluctuations in the market are inevitabilities we all have to welcome. In the rental property business achieving the 'super-survivor' survivor status calls for more user creativity to better perform market analysis checks.

Ensure constant feeds from rental-pricing comparisons, knowing what's baking around in terms of apartment upgrades, and having the keen eye on cap rates in the rental property sphere. Pay heed, my friend, because these practices not only give you backbone solid prompts on a daily, monthly but they could unabashedly secure you more rent, value enhancement, and sustained Tenant-occupancy.

3. Resilient negotiation Skills

Let me tell ya, my friend, the rental property venture isn't all about smile-crossed greetings and finalizing deals. Property purchases, management service fee-bargains hinge on effective negotiation. Be ever-ready to wear the resistance belt of resilience during your rental property negotiations for better compromises on interests.

4. Continuum Learning Ghost

Despite purchasing your A-to-Z's book of the rental property business before you cartwheel into the pond, let the pursuit of knowledge be your ghost. With evolving state housing laws, rental rights, tenant-screening ideals, the real estate runway is incessantly introducing fresh fashion.

Transcend your "Good enough" looking picture. Proactively reinvent yourself towards industry growth peaks using experts' webinars, podcasts, books, and even an old employee's anecdotes can be a valuable peg from which to hang your expectations, especially if you're starting from scratch.

5. Emotional endurance

Every shifting wave on the pond leaves a ripple. Trivial fluctuations in your rental business can often cause giant stressful ripples. Stress on smaller hitches or maxed-out emergencies happens. Rather than panicking, fuel all hitches with a solution magnetized approach. Staying calm, even in the choppy waters of financial crisis or market declivity is the thumb safety rule.

6. Mind-Environment balance protocol.

Yes, taking environmental accountability form in the rental property venture isn't just your moral obligation but an undeniable identity. Instituting measures to offer a more eco-green environment means savings on utility rates and command potential tenant boomerang throws.

Consider integrating sustainable practices like recycling, energy-efficient gadgets bulb fixture lighting, water saver implementations, and pollinator-friendly spaces. Bottom line? –As an investor in rental property, protect Mother Nature, her way and enjoy maximized returns!

Stepping onto the rental property play-barn can be convoluted, teeming with obstacles from financial inadequacies, constant market shifts, to state property-law-tangles, okay, feel my virtual wink? But your journey can morph from trippy to a confident skip with these tabled strategies sooner than you imagine.

My friend, consistently reminding yourself of progress points and opportunities in the pipeline with the buoyant art of consistency can make significant strides towards long-term rental property venture piece of grail to covet.

Beat challenge beast with alacrity and impeccable strategy, but never forget the bliss springing on consistent vision fueling sessions empowering motivation keep at-top fervor gear.

Now, be a gladiator, augment the spectral knowledge on your rental property business venture, seasoned spiced even amidst birthing difficulties. Applying the input correctly unlocks potential higher rental output doors, while decked additionally in adventure, would you deny? Thoughts abound, but remember, my friend showing up relentlessly is more first-man-action towards most progressive progress path.

Maintaining motivation and persistence in rental property investing

I wanted to talk to you about something that we don't always discuss in depth: the rental property business. It has its fair share of challenges, but trust me… where there are challenges, there's also opportunity. With the right guidance and mindset, you can make rental property investing a successful venture. So, pull up a chair, this is going to be a long chat. Grab a cup of coffee or, heck, glass of wine. Whichever suits you are fine by me.

Ironing Out the Challenges

Just so we're on the same page, let me jot down some of the common challenges that often discourage budding investors. Screening quality tenants, unexpected maintenance costs, market and economic fluctuations, management hassles, and in-depth knowledge of local laws and ordinances can all add to your plate…and it's already filled pretty high. But hey, don't let me bury this under a ton of boulders just yet. Every cloud has a silver lining. Let's explore how to conquer these, shall we?

Screening Quality Tenants

Picking the right tenant can be a nightmare. The ideal tenant pays on time, keeps the property tidy, and ensures that problems are promptly reported. Unfortunately, life isn't always generous with these unheard creatures.

To make the screening process smoother, give credit checks, employment verification, and reference checklists a shot. Invest a decent chunk of time—it's worth it. Document everything to shield yourself from potential lawsuits and show the shiny ribbons of the law, should it come to calling up the path.

Unexpected Maintenance Costs

Imagine, right when you think everything is smooth sailing, you get a call that your rental's dishwasher has gone rogue, endangering those poor, defenseless dishes. With ownership come these unexpected issues begging for your attention.

To tackle this, apart from having a Madam Faultfinder or her cousin, Mr. Handyman on speed dial, make sure you build an emergency fund. It acts as a buffer that comes to your rescue in emergencies.

Finally, regular inspections buddy. Don't forget ever!

Constant Market Fluctuation

The state of the economy affects rental prices. During fresh fragrant times, life can be peaches. But during a crisis, rent prices might shrink down just taller than a blade of grass, or even crumble up all together. And my friend, brace yourself - mark such times on your calendar.

When dealing with uncertain economic times, the best thing to do is stay patient and flexible. Lowering your rents may be a better move than running into void periods.

Complete Knowledge of Rental Laws

Local laws have surprising twists and turns like the spine of some creepy monsters. Some areas have notorious strict housing regulations while others ride a rather relaxed tractor.

Dedicate yourself to learning local laws and regulations. Without this knowledge, you might shuffle ahead into pretty risky revelations. Nor would anyone be prepared with a toast to your disbelief.

The Power of Positiveness: Staying Motivated

Now to our cupcake icing–Staying Motivated. Most things hop onto you famished, do put up a tough fight. Here are some tips and bits I've learned.

Continuously remind yourself of the initial reasons behind starting this endeavor. Was it for financial independence? To build a legacy for your children, perhaps? Keep your why alive - it coupled with victory can storm through many barriers.

Celebrate your small victories. Closed your first deal? Awesome! Was able to resolve a maintenance issue effectively? Fantastic! This will keep you going even through the thorns that linger undefeatable.

Use the problem to water growth. It might sound funny, but in this business, you gotta dance your win with what pulls you down. Stare at it deep in the eye and smirk, "Well, nice try." The challenges you experience equip you better for the next mighty course.

Chapter 25: Conclusion and Action Plan

Recap of key concepts and strategies for rental income

How Do You Get the Most Out of Your $Rental Invested Bucks$?

Well buddy, here we are at the end of the road. We've surfed from finding just the right property for investment to curating our own landlord-self or blooming a savvy property manager; we ambled through tax benefits right down to the expedition of so many wealth-boosting benefits rental properties offered.

But, what's left? Action plans for getting that villa in the Bahamas? High five buddy!! Let's weave the final masterpiece: conclude the points and frame the utter guide towards a convivial rental income life!

In case you had skim-read it (please don't pretend I can't see you peeking), this is the climax scene: RECAP-TIME!

So…how do we even define Rental Income?

Hey, please stop drumming your fingers at the calculator after looking at your fancy new apartment thinking— 'Rental income equals lazily-attained property-related-payoff'!

Rental Income, my friend, equals ALL amounts you received as rent. Long-story short, total rental bucks; total-pay-off= fiscal-mouth-watering-Benes plus benevolent-benefits.

Phew! Got that out of the sparkling way.

There's always bulging 'super-punch-profit' options round the alley. But don't get your nerves scrambled trying to seize 'em all. Let's pour galore light on some key strategies meant to elevate-rocket your blood-shot rental income!

Enhancing Property Condition: 'Fidelity-hysters', 'a-classers' consider property-value 'Bonnie'. Just like a royal Victorian castle grabs millionaire mogul—property condition utilizes the same magnet! Improved properties => Higher quality tenants.

Bit o' decor, add amenities-gone-classy Swanky-designed => Epic-dollars, Capisci? Negotiating Lease Terms: Hell, I could rent for an-absolute-season and ditch when I seize a profitable dwelling path. But Security=>Set-rental. Planning to send chirruping songbirds long-term contract singing=>sticking around. Remember, long-term lease to apartment value recession is as stubborn tail light during a hot car chase as reliable tenants during downturns!

Cognizance Shift: Writing this cozy-couch-buddy, I earnestly desire you to enjoy the flavor of Value offerings over meagre survival price-counter. Tax deductibility and the glamorous accessorizing-score-pricing can concoct wickedly-splendid pricing punch.

Flying feathers! These truckloads keynotes pinning hopes, ecstatic yet? Wait up for the end-zinger!

Balancing Act: Profit Magnets with Liability-light

Calculating cost vs turnover doesn't involve witty wizardry but plain safety-paranormal keeping checks! Offering services while keeping purchases wrapped ensures clean calculation-slates keeping financial health and mental peace chatting in sync.

Think double before guarantee-services; negotiations, prudent-renovation timing and contingency budget for on-text shenanigans. With a good chunk of savings stashed into realty slices, you're sitting on a bulky-profit-couch!

Cocktail mixture – Wealth-x-renter's delight: Satisfy tenant demands heartily, real-bucks tag along surefootedly. Consistent attention to detail both property-wise and people-pleasure-wise offers promising potential for both wealth and well-deserved patron reputation-patronage!

Road's end –time! Did you decide your rental jungle or marathon brewing uphill profits yet?

Ready to roll the Action-plan-canvas?

Let this confession pen lead you throughout $$$ journey smoother than betting glass-slippers to pumpkin-curtains minus squall-frustration. Translate hindsight to instant clear-neon signposting results.

Hang Warm 'Welcome'== Consistent Casual-bucks : Safe-habitat show-empathy guarantees permanent occupancy leasing out beautiful words— 'rent-regulation'.

Long Lease Duration==Tumbled Cash : You already gained a bird's eye glimpse that Security=high pay dirt due to fixed-rental opportunity.

Swanky Swing makes Luxury Ring : Metaphor? Luxury seducing lifestyle combined with rental sprinklers invoke big leagues pick-up sticks.

Fee-offer Paints Gold : Security-deposit add-ons lay fortunate-ball games—elevating weekly check reality deep till last $$ payouts— if played deftly!

Statistically Enroll— Digitally Swing & Roll : Hi-tech uptake because online-realty market swings more comfy-addictive towards younger demographic market share insights undoubtedly golf high.

Creating a personalized action plan for rental property investing success

Setting Your Objectives

First things first. The voyage is futile without determining a destination. What do you achieve from your rental property investments? Steady flow of cash, additional income or strategic retirement planning? Pin down your objectives to lure the perfect opportunities from market haywire.

Understanding the Market

You know how we used to research the opponents before our weekend match-ups. We are going to do exactly the same. Question - what you truly wish in your investment? A modest house offering promising cash flow, classic suburban multiplex, or windfall generating trendy condo downtown? Your goal will surely sync with a specific type of asset. Research neighborhoods, gather information about the rental market like median rents, tenant turnover, vacancy rates to consolidate your view.

Planning your Financial Commitment

How can we miss talking about money here? After all, enjoyment requires expenditure. Is rental property investment something alien? Decide your financial strength? Are you into leveraging or using up the lump sum? Calculation based around asset price, mortgage, renovation, Insurance, taxes might feel like solving a Rubix cube but that's the drill - an essential one! Employ proficient advisor if required but without bearing clear vision is risky like betting blind folded.

Rental Management

Friend, ever realized being a landlord not just needs potential to purchase but also using it profitably. Are you prepared getting the call middle of the night - your tenant has an emergency leak? Possibly not! Consider bringing professional property manager onboard. You'd be acquiring peace at the cost of their fee but isn't your sanity priceless?

Mark a Benchmark

Bingo! Your blueprint appears more like reality now. Understand achieving investment objectives is a continuous process demanding constant evaluation. Specific goals framed in terms of key performance indicators will assist throughout the journey. Concurrently, tracking the progress stands imperative. Therefore, akin to our pre-game planning - touch your feets on groundwork, warm-up through extensive preparation, strategize your moves, ultimately dash the arena with confidence and emerge victorious - its similar set up. Just be particular over your goal, contain your excitement during upheavals and tediousness shall evaporate like morning mist on a summer morning!

I appreciate, prepping up this personalized commandment might feel onerous yet summing up white papers out there provided challenges as well. Show me any endeavor claiming utmost authenticity excluding toil and difficulty, my friend. Every goal, invariably shines brightest reward only when carved out with organization and determination. So, feeling ready donning the property mogul hat? Then let's get the ball rolling because everything waits but time.

Tips for Maximizing Rental Property Income

Set competitive rental rates to attract tenants.

Market your rental property online through various listing platforms.

Advertise your property in local newspapers and community boards.

Offer incentives to potential tenants, such as discounted rent for the first month.

Maintain a well-maintained and clean property to attract quality tenants.

Screen potential tenants thoroughly to avoid problematic renters.

Consider offering furnished rental options for higher rental rates.

Implement a late rent fee policy to ensure timely payments.

Offer long-term lease agreements to provide stability and reduce turnover.

Utilize social media platforms to promote your rental property.

Consider renting out storage spaces or parking spots to increase income.

Offer pet-friendly rental options to attract a larger pool of tenants.

Utilize professional property management services to handle tenant concerns and maintenance.

Consider renting out individual rooms in a larger property for higher rental income.

Install energy-efficient appliances and fixtures to reduce utility costs.

Offer online rent payment options to streamline the payment process.

Consider renting out your property as a vacation rental for higher short-term rental rates.

Offer additional services such as cleaning or maintenance for an additional fee.

Consider renting out your property for events or photo shoots for extra income.

Invest in properties located near popular attractions or universities for higher rental demand.

Offer flexible lease terms, such as month-to-month options, to attract a wider range of tenants.

Implement a referral program for current tenants to encourage them to bring in new tenants.

Consider offering rent-to-own options for tenants looking to become homeowners.

Implement a preventative maintenance schedule to avoid costly repairs in the long run.

Offer online tour options for potential tenants who may not be able to visit in person.

Utilize professional photography to showcase your property in online listings.

Offer amenities such as a gym, pool, or laundry facilities to attract tenants.

Consider offering short-term rental options for travelers or business professionals.

Negotiate lower property taxes to reduce expenses and increase profitability.

Stay up to date with local rental market trends to adjust rental rates accordingly.

Network with other landlords or property investors to learn about potential investment opportunities.

Consider offering rent concessions or discounts during slow rental periods to attract tenants.

Implement an efficient tenant turnover process to minimize vacancy periods.

Offer online maintenance request options to streamline the repair process.

Consider offering renter's insurance options to tenants for added protection.

Offer flexible payment options, such as weekly or bi-weekly rent payments.

Implement a tenant loyalty program to encourage long-term tenants to stay.

Consider investing in properties with multiple units for higher rental income.

Offer online lease signing options to simplify the leasing process.

Invest in property upgrades or renovations to attract higher-paying tenants.

Consider offering additional services such as landscaping or snow removal for an additional fee.

To guarantee dependable and accountable tenants, establish a thorough tenant screening process.

Regularly review and adjust rental rates to match market demand.

Offer incentives for tenants to renew their lease, such as a rent discount or upgraded amenities.

Utilize professional property staging services to showcase your rental property.

Offer flexible move-in dates to accommodate potential tenants' schedules.

Consider partnering with local businesses for exclusive discounts or perks for your tenants.

Offer online tenant portals for easy communication and access to important documents.

Consider investing in properties with potential for value appreciation for long-term profitability.

Regularly inspect and maintain the property to avoid costly repairs and keep tenants satisfied.

Milton Keynes UK
Ingram Content Group UK Ltd.
UKHW010241221123
432980UK00002B/234